HEAVEN
IN ORDINARY

*Contemplative Prayer
in Ordinary Life*

ANGELA ASHWIN

McCRIMMON
Great Wakering Essex England

For Clare, Tim and Andrew

First published in 1985 by
Mayhew McCrimmon Ltd
Great Wakering Essex England
Reprinted 1986, 1988, 1989

ISBN 0 85597 380 3

Cover design and lithographic artwork: Nick Snode
Typesetting: Phoenix Typesetters Ltd, Southend-on-Sea, Essex
Printed by Mayhew-McCrimmon Printers, Great Wakering, Essex

Contents

PART THREE
Pain and failure

PART FOUR
What can I offer?

Preface

I owe a tremendous amount to the inspiration and support of many friends in the writing of this book. In particular I am grateful to Father Simon Holden, CR, for his wisdom and guidance. I would also like to thank the Revd Nick Beddow and Mrs Christine Blakesley for their practical assistance, and the many good friends with whom I have talked hard and long about the questions which I am exploring.

The greatest debt of all is to my husband, Vincent. For a long time he has put up with a house full of scraps of paper containing 'thoughts for the book'. Without his deep understanding and help of all kinds, this book would not have been possible.

My title is taken from the poem 'Prayer' by George Herbert, in *The English Poems of George Herbert,* edited by C. A. Patrides (Dent, London, 1974). The original spelling is 'Heaven in ordinarie'.

Unless otherwise stated, all Bible references are taken from the Revised Standard Version, Second Edition, 1971.

Introduction

How can we possibly live prayerfully, centred in the stillness of God, when our days are full of activity and noise? It seems a hopeless task.

After several years of struggling with this question, reading, and talking to others, I have found some guidelines which I hope to share with those who feel drawn towards the contemplative life in a busy world.

I realise how very much I am a beginner in all that I have said. I write not as an expert, but as a fellow-seeker in the infinitely exciting and compelling adventure of life with God.

Angela Ashwin
Shildon, Co Durham
Advent 1984

Part one
Can I live a life of prayer?

1. I'm not free

Prayerful people are often busy people, but they have a serenity about them which is part of their effectiveness. — John Dalrymple.

Great figures like Mother Theresa of Calcutta have given their lives to prayer and the service of the poor. Monks and nuns have a rhythm of worship and silence built into the pattern of their life, so that they are able to spend many hours in stillness with God.

But most of us are simply not free to devote long hours to prayer every day, or to uproot ourselves and go to serve Christ in the remote parts of the world. Our work or our family absorb most of our time and attention, so that we are tempted to think that the life of prayer and silence and total self-giving to God is not for us.

Yet the fact that we are busy people with all kinds of commitments is not necessarily a death sentence for our spiritual life. There is a calling to which we are *all* free to respond. It is as real as a vocation to enter a monastery or convent, and just as vital in the life of God's people on earth. We are called to be totally given to Christ at every moment, in a completely ordinary situation.

A wide-eyed lady in conversation with a Franciscan friar once said: 'Oh, but you have chosen the higher way,' thus consigning the rest of us to second class citizenship of the kingdom of heaven. To live a life of prayer, we do not have to play at being monks and nuns, dashing off to say Divine Offices in the spare room every few hours. For an office worker, teacher or housewife there are other patterns of prayer which do work, and are hidden and flexible. There are ways of finding stillness with God, even in the noisy world of rush hours, meetings and family life.

At one time 'contemplation' was seen as a special form of union with God, reserved only for the most outstanding people if they were lucky enough to be on the receiving end. Now more and more Christians are realising that contemplative prayer — by which we mean inner stillness with God — is open to anyone.

A vocation does not only lead to a dog collar or a habit. It is the definite vocation of many people to live contemplatively in an ordinary home or job. Praying is not therefore something we manage *in spite of* our everyday life; we live prayerfully *in* and *because of* our situation. It is a sad waste of opportunity if we leave the serious attempts at praying to the special people.

★ ★ ★ ★ ★

There are days when every available moment seems to be filled. After a demanding day at work there may hardly be time to snatch something to eat before dashing off to an evening commitment. A mother of young children can spend the whole day finding scissors and paint, clearing up the mess, answering questions, and doing bits of housework when she has a chance.

A busy life can be immensely frustrating, because there appears to be no chance to stop and pray. We feel like giving up altogether, and putting off any thoughts of prayer until later — perhaps until we have changed our job, or the children are older, or at least until church on Sunday (if we can get there). We forget that every moment is God's moment; the kingdom of heaven is here, in the factory and the lecture room and the kitchen. This is where I can say: 'Yes, Lord, I am Yours, here and now,' in the middle of it all.

We are called to give ourselves to God *today* as well as next month. There is nothing to stop us praying right in the thick of our busiest moments. A simple prayer such as 'Abba, Father' offered in a queue at the railway ticket office or supermarket can be the first step of an adventure into inward communion with God which will affect everything we do and are.

★ ★ ★ ★ ★

The kingdom of God is in the midst of you. (Luke 17:21)

2. It helps to be ordinary

The first lesson we have to learn about prayer ... is that it is
God's activity in us and not a self-activated process of our
own. — Mother Mary Clare, SLG.

It is an advantage not to be famous or important. Well known
Christians have to cope with the world's admiration and criticism,
which can both make prayer and inward simplicity ten times harder.
Obviously God works through church leaders and in big missions and
rallies. But He also needs the quiet and inconspicuous lives of the
millions of Christians who make up the vast majority of His people on
earth.

The reason why it helps to be ordinary is that as Christians we
depend on God and not on ourselves. The heart of contemplative
prayer is being empty before God in simplicity and stillness, so that
He has room to work in us. It is much easier to be receptive towards
God if we are neither famous nor important. Popularity and power
could quickly become a blockage, making us depend on ourselves
rather than God, and cluttering us up with pride and ambition.

The great Christian saints have always managed to preserve their
total dependence on God, in spite of public praise. For most of us this
particular struggle is not such a problem, so we should perhaps be
thankful that we are just ordinary people.

★ ★ ★ ★ ★

Michael and Jill are both teachers who have come to live in a new
area. They join the local church, and the congregation are delighted to
welcome this 'lovely young couple' into their midst. Jill is invited to
give a talk to the Over-Sixties' Club, and senses that they all think she
is marvellous. Michael has been appointed deputy head at the local
school, and most parents are rather in awe of him. Jill and Michael

both become involved in work for a local charity, and someone says to them: 'You do so much for God, I don't know how you fit it all in.'

All this popularity and praise is very pleasant, but it makes prayer quite difficult for Michael and Jill. They know that they have made quite an impact in the community; everything they do seems to go well. It is a struggle to hang on to their dependence on God, and to say with conviction: 'Lord, we are nothing; You are all.'

Then the first baby arrives! Jill comes home from hospital exhausted after a string of sleepless nights in a noisy ward. She feeds and changes the baby, and hopes that he will settle. But he cries and yells, showing no sign of sleeping. Suddenly Michael and Jill panic as the huge responsibility of having a new child hits them. Still the baby cries.

Frantically they search in baby-care books to find out what to do next. Then a kind neighbour calls. Michael answers with the baby in one arm and *Doctor Spock* in the other. The neighbour takes one look at Jill's drained and tear-stained face and says: 'Let me take the baby for the night. One bottle-feed won't do him any harm.' Jill nods gratefully and sinks into bed for a badly needed sleep.

During the first few weeks of the baby's life, Michael and Jill have to rely on friends for a good deal of help. This is a turning point in their prayer. There is a sort of release, now that people have seen that they cannot always cope, and that they are as liable to get into a flap as anybody else.

Now Michael and Jill find it easier to be themselves with God, and realise their need of Him in a new way. They also see the funny side of their helplessness. That is always a good foundation for prayer.

★   ★   ★   ★   ★

How blest are those who know their need of God; the kingdom of Heaven is theirs. (Matt 5:3. NEB, 1970 edition)

3. We don't feel worthy

For my part, the only insight I have is into my own little
nothingness. And this does more for me than new insights on
the Faith. — St Thérèse of Lisieux.

A reason frequently given for not bothering with any kind of spiritual
life is that people feel unworthy. It is thought that you have to be
somehow 'respectable' or 'virtuous' in order to be religious. Many
people genuinely feel that their life is so full of shortcomings that it
would be false or hypocritical to seek a way of contemplative prayer:

'How can I even presume to try and live prayerfully when I spend
all day feeling exasperated and critical about the people I work with?'

'I'm too old to start praying now; I've never lived a good enough
life anyway.'

'I've done nothing but shout at the children all day. I would feel a
hypocrite if I sat down and prayed now.'

Those who say this have got entirely the wrong end of the stick!
None of us is worthy. We are all selfish and unkind at times. We do not
strictly deserve God's love, but we receive it nonetheless.

Whoever thinks that he or she *is* worthy has probably missed the
heart of the Gospel, by being too preoccupied with achievement and
merit. It was one of the mistakes of the Pharisees to assume that they
could score enough points of virtue to gain entry into the kingdom of
God. We never earn God's mercy and love; they are freely given.

Much of life is a struggle, with a good deal of failure. Most people
who pray would say that a large part of their prayer is muddled and
distracted. Yet in a sense failure doesn't matter. What does matter is if
we stop trying. That is the danger point.

The great temptation is to despair and give up following Christ and praying, because we feel we cannot do it. But *we* can never do it! Which of us can say: 'I've done it! I'm worthy! Here I am, Lord, the Super Saint You always wanted!'

If we persevere in our efforts to live prayerfully, we will still make blunders. But we will also be surprised by the power of God's goodness to do in us the things we least expected.

★ ★ ★ ★ ★

It often takes someone extraordinary to teach us something about being ordinary.

Dag Hammarskjöld's career appeared as a string of successes from the outside. He moved rapidly through the worlds of finance and government service to become Secretary General of the United Nations in 1953. His inner spiritual life was hidden from the world until his personal reflections were published after his death in 1961, under the title *Markings*[1]. These jottings reveal the depths of suffering and self examination in Hammarskjöld's interior life, especially his struggles with ambition and pride.

In many ways he felt totally unworthy of the enormous responsibility which had been given to him: 'It is not the repeated mistakes, the long succession of petty betrayals — though, God knows, they would give cause enough for anxiety and self-contempt — but the huge elementary mistake, the betrayal of that within me which is greater than I ... (p57). '... Never let success hide its emptiness from you, achievement its nothingness ...' (p63).

He eventually found a way through that sense of unworthiness, in the longing 'to *live,* to know that in God I am nothing, but that God is in me' (p88).

He saw that he was nothing more than an instrument of God: 'How humble the tool when praised for what the hand has done.'

His image of the lens could apply to any Christian: 'You are merely the lens in the beam. You can only receive, give and possess the light as a lens does' (p133).

The years in which his faith and prayer had deepened so profoundly were those spent in the ruthless world of international rivalries and diplomacy. He discovered his total dependence on God in all this, through the knowledge of his own weakness and nothingness. We need to learn the same lesson in our mundane and unspectacular circumstances.

The very unworthiness that we had considered such a barrier to our spiritual life is the point where we realise how much we need God's mercy and love. It is when we make this discovery that things start to happen.

★ ★ ★ ★ ★

Lord, I am part of the pain and sin of the world.
     Come into the world's tension, in which I share;
     Heal the world's resentment, of which I am a part;
     forgive the world's selfishness, to which I contribute.
I offer You my unworthiness and sadness: take them up into
     Your great work of healing and redeeming mankind.

✳ ✳ ✳ ✳ ✳

But God shows His love for us in that while we were yet sinners Christ died for us. (Romans 5:8)

NOTES

1. Faber, 1964.

4. God doesn't only want the 'holy' bits of life

The more you believe in the Incarnation the more you care
about drains. — Henry Scott-Holland.

The glory of God is man fully alive, and the life of man is the
vision of God. — Irenaeus.

The Christian life is not a separate compartment, boxed away from
ordinary activities, an optional extra which we fit in if we have a space
somewhere. People sometimes think that divine and earthly things
cannot possibly mix. Some say that Christianity is only concerned
with saving souls; social, economic and political life don't appear to
have much to do with it. Or else the secular worlds of business,
industry and leisure seem to be utterly remote from religion and
'churchy' activities.

But God is not thousands of miles away, only paying us a visit on
Sundays. He is in His world, in its profoundest depths and minutest
details, and in the heart of every pain. God in Jesus has become *flesh*.
So, as well as being wholly other than we are, beyond our human
comprehension, God is also here with us in the middle of it all, inviting
us to respond and work with Him.

God calls us to be totally given to Him in everything, from the way
we spend our money to the way we talk to other people. It doesn't
matter whether we are washing the car, interviewing clients or giving
the children their tea — God is still there, and we can still be
surrendered to Him at those moments.

But how? The secret lies in prayer, which is possible wherever we
are. God doesn't only want the 'holy bits' of our weekly routine. All of
life can be sacred if we will only look and listen.

* * * * *

Somebody I know was thinking about ordination in the Church of England ministry, when he realised that God was calling him to serve Christ in a totally secular environment. So he found a job in the junior management of a large firm, and was eventually promoted to the position of personnel officer. He was often misunderstood and criticised both by management and shop stewards in his role as peacemaker. Much of his time was spent in listening, and trying to enable people to find fulfilment in their particular kind of work. His life could be exhausting and costly, as well as exciting. Although his job had none of the usual religious labels, his role was essentially Christ-like. Through prayer, his life with God and his work in the factory were one.

* * * * *

As a teenager I went to a disco in a church hall. During the evening we noticed a figure of Christ on the cross hanging on the wall. This seemed almost incongruous in the middle of the throbbing music and flashing lights. But why should a crucifix be out of place at a dance? Wasn't Christ there too? Perhaps it seemed somehow irreverent. Yet the gifts of music and rhythm and colour came from God in the first place!

Do we think that God is not interested in what we do in our spare time? We make Him sound so prim and proper by our narrow ideas! Perhaps the Lord of the Dance was dancing there too that night.

* * * * *

And the Word became flesh, and dwelt among us. (John 1:14)

5. We can pray all the time

Make frequent aspirations to God by short but ardent movements of your heart; admire His beauty, implore His assistance, cast yourself at the foot of the Cross, adore His goodness, converse with Him a thousand times a day. — St Francis de Sales.

There must be spaces at some time or another when we do nothing but pray, dropping everything else in order to be alone with God (see next section). But prayer does not end there. Our conversation with God does not have to come to an abrupt close when we emerge from our fifteen or twenty minutes with a Bible.

We may know in theory that we could pray in any situation; but most of us actually *do* so surprisingly little. The main reason is that we are busy planning what jobs to do, or thinking about a problem, or just day dreaming. We may cast the occasional glance in God's direction, but, if we are honest, huge chunks of our life are prayerless.

Some people do not pray while they are working because they assume that all prayer should be cast in traditional church language. Finding appropriate words seems too much of an effort when they are in the middle of doing other things. They do not realise that it is possible to chat to God in our own words. God wants us to relax and be ourselves with Him. It is not irreverent to natter to Him about everything on our minds, or to tell Him exactly how we feel. If we want to grumble, it is best to grumble to God. This is prayer, just as much as the beautiful language of church and prayer books. Posh vocabulary is not necessary! It is useless to try to put on a respectable face specially for God: we cannot fool Him, because He knows us inside out. If Jesus had wanted us to talk to God in strictly formal language, He would not have taught us to approach God as 'Abba, Father'. The closest translation we can make of that is 'Daddy'.

If we talk to God often enough, it becomes a habit. Then God starts to open up to us new ways of praying, attracting us into a deeper and deeper love of Him.

★　★　★　★　★

'Lord, please help me to get through today. I'm dreading this afternoon; people can be so difficult. Lord, give me patience!' There will be days when all our prayers are like this. At other times we may be exhilarated by the glorious freshness and colour of the world, or delighted by some good news. Then prayer will reflect our happiness and excitement. Possibilities for prayer are endless.

When somebody comes into the office or rings the front doorbell, we could pray that the person who is there will see something of Christ in us. If we are stuck in a traffic jam, our frustration can be offered as an intercession for those who really are 'stuck' — imprisoned and tortured for what they believe to be right, or helplessly tangled up in a web of economic disaster and poverty. Preparing meals can be a time when we pray for the poor who are unable to feed their own children. Listening to music can be a springboard for thankfulness. A saintly old lady in Africa confesses her sins with gusto as she vigorously rubs the dirt out of the family washing. Removing the mud from a pair of football boots could provide a similar opportunity for penance!

The more we pray like this, the more new ideas come for all sorts of praying during the day.

★　★　★　★　★

Rejoice alway; pray without ceasing, in everything give thanks. (I Thess 5:16-17, RV)

6. A word to hang on to

Take a short word . . . the shorter the better, being more like
the working of the Spirit! A word like GOD or LOVE.
Choose which you like, or perhaps some other . . . and fix
this word fast to your heart, so that it is always there come
what may. — 14th-century anonymous writer.

Adopt a short word! Or, rather, let it adopt you. A short prayer or
phrase which means a lot to us can become a good companion during
the day, if we repeat it constantly to ourselves. It could be called a
'word friend'. Using a word or phrase like this enables us to move from
chatting with God to being with Him on a deeper level. This is another
aspect of the mysterious business of praying without ceasing —
'mysterious' because God begins to take over more and more, leading
us into unknown territories of communion with Him.

There are many different kinds of 'word friend'. Some people use
'arrow prayers', the short aspirations that we can shoot up to God at
any time. Words which suit one person will not always help another.
Mrs X may say, 'Lord, I am Yours', while Mr Z prefers to pray,
'Abba, Father'. We each have to find the words which are right for us.

The Orthodox Church has the great tradition of saying the 'Jesus
Prayer' (Lord, Jesus Christ, Son of God, have mercy on me, a sinner).
If we repeat these words many times, they sink into the unconscious
and bring the depths of the soul into a unique knowledge of Jesus's
forgiveness and presence.

Another source of words and phrases is a daily Bible passage. As we
read it, we may come to a particular sentence which strikes us, and
which we can take with us through the day. We have a good
companion.

The repeated words bring our mind back to God when we have become distracted and harassed. Something else happens, too. As the words sink into us, they release God's healing energy into deep-seated hurts and tensions.

On some days life is so impossible that there is no chance to snatch a few minutes to read a Bible passage. If you have to drive a long way for an urgent appointment, and start out at crack of dawn, or if you are woken at 5am by a child who is about to be sick, you may well have no chance to stop for a quiet time. On days like this a short prayer comes to your rescue, and remains a good friend. If you use a daily Bible reading scheme which gives a single verse as well as a longer passage (eg in the *Letter from Taizé*[1]) you can take that verse with you to make even the most demanding day God-centred.

The Bible is bursting with imagery that can take root inside us. If, for example, we adopt the word 'yeast' or 'shepherd' or 'living water', the image can grow in us, so that we deepen our understanding of it during the day. God may also use that word to work in us in ways we are not aware of at the time.

'Word friends' can come from any source, not just the Bible. They could be found in any book or hymn, or in a talk or sermon.

Words are never ends in themselves, but are only signposts which point to the infinite, to God. If we think that we can grasp or contain Him in *any* set of words, all we are left with is an empty shell. God is far greater than any concepts or ideas about Him.

We must let the words live and breathe in us, so that our spirit and the eternal Spirit of God somehow touch each other. Then the words have done their job. They have directed us beyond themselves, leading to a peaceful communion with God which is beyond any words. We cannot comprehend, but we can love.

★　★　★　★　★

How do we know which words to choose?

Straining and scratching around to find the appropriate word will never yield results. We have to relax and let go of our furious search, so that we are open and ready to receive the word or words which speak to us at that particular time. We will find the right prayer or phrase soon enough. In practice, we may use one word for two or three days or weeks without changing. At other times we may move to a new one every day. God deals with us all differently. If we are inwardly receptive and flexible, putting ourselves in His hands, we can trust Him to guide us.

It is good to have a basic word, a life time friend, to which we can always return on days when nothing else is given. (Some people have just one word for life in any case.) The name of 'Jesus', or simply 'Father', both take a lot of beating.

Some examples
This is only a smattering of the vast range of possibilities. Each person must wait and receive what God wants to give.

Arrow Prayers
Jesus
Father
Abba, Father
Christ
Lord
Love
My shepherd
Lord, I love you
Lord, help me
Lord, I trust You
Lord, forgive me
Lord Jesus Christ, Son of God, have mercy on me
Jesus, live in me
Yes, Lord

Words and phrases from the Bible
Mercy
Glory
Light
Peace
My rock
Bread of life
Forgiven
Your sins are forgiven
In Thee O Lord I put my trust
Into Your hands I commend my spirit
Fear not
This is My beloved Son
He is risen
Take up your cross
Unless a seed fall and die
My grace is sufficient
Abide in me and I in you

I am with you always

Simon (insert your own name) do you love me?

Sentences from other sources

Love was his meaning (Mother Julian of Norwich)

Contemplation is where the soul meets the infinite (Ladislaus Boros)

Life is only for love (St Bernard)

God is the friend of silence (Mother Theresa of Calcutta)

Lead, kindly light (Cardinal Newman)

Let go and let God (Anon)

Love bade me welcome (George Herbert)

My God and my all (St Francis of Assissi)

All shall be well and all shall be well and all manner of thing shall be well (Mother Julian)

* * * * *

Thy word is a lamp to my feet, and a light to my path. (Psalm 119 v.105)

NOTES

1. *Letter from Taizé,* 71250 Taizé Community, France

7. Spaces for praying are given to us

Unless there is a still centre in the middle of the storm,
unless a man in the midst of all his activities preserves a
secret room in his heart, where he stands alone before God,
then he will lose all sense of spiritual direction, and be torn
to pieces. — Kallistos Ware.

If we love a person very much, we need to be alone with them
sometimes. It is not enough just to be with them in a crowd, and to
think about them while we are busy working. The relationship will be
starved unless we can find times to enjoy each other's company
undisturbed. It is the same with God. Chatting to Him throughout the
day is not a substitute for specific periods of quiet with Him, but is just
another part of the *whole* life of prayer. We still need times when we do
nothing but pray. It is impossible to continue a deeply loving
relationship with God unless we sometimes leave everything else on
one side, in order just to be with Him. The trouble is that a busy life
makes it difficult to fit in times like this. Yet there must be a way.

The obvious guide is Jesus Himself. In spite of the huge demands
made on Him, He still managed to spend periods alone with God. He
lived in a rhythm of involvement and withdrawal, busyness and
solitude, which is at the heart of the contemplative way of life.

It is often thought that our quiet-times must be at exactly the same
point every day. But Jesus didn't manage that. It is clear from the
gospels that He was not able to have a set time for daily prayer.
Clamouring crowds, long journeys, and the need to preach and heal,
all prevented such a pattern. But when the time was *given*, Jesus took
it. That was the key: 'Great crowds gathered to hear Him and to be
cured of their ailments. And from time to time He would withdraw to
lonely places for prayer ... During this time He went out one day into
the hills to pray, and spent the night in prayer to God ...' (Luke 5:15-
16, and 6:12, NEB)

When we are trying to find time and opportunity to be quiet with God, it can be extremely frustrating. Some days there is literally no chance except very late at night, when we are so tired that we fall asleep. We feel like giving up altogether, because it seems that there will never be a chance to stop and pray. But this does not have to be so. The secret is to treat the time for prayer as something given. A free ten minutes falls into our lap for us to use if we are willing; it is a gift rather than a space which we wrench out of our packed schedule and begrudgingly give to God.

The gap between prayer-times may be thirty-six hours or more; but that is irrelevant as long as we accept the opportunities to pray when they do come. It makes sense to promise that the first free ten or twenty minutes which come to us, whenever that may be, will be used for nothing but prayer. Some people can manage a longer time than this, and many have more than one period for prayer in a day. That is a matter between God and ourselves.

There is a sense of freedom when we make this our rule of life. It is like travelling by rail. Once you have stepped onto a train, you have handed over your movement to someone else. The train carries you and you are free to use the time of the journey without having to think about where you are going. There is the same kind of freedom with this discipline of prayer. Once we have promised our first free space to God, we can relax and stop straining to fit in a prayer-time. It will be given and, when that moment comes, we will take it.

* * * * *

Yet this is easier said than done. It is surprising how tempting it is to ignore the opportunity to pray when it does arise. In the mornings I often have a chance to be alone with God while the children are at school. But the breakfast dishes need washing up, and then I must hoover downstairs, put the washing machine on and go shopping. It is a real struggle to let go of all this for a moment and sit down and pray, while I'm looking at the cornflakes stuck to the sides of the cereal bowls. I am pulled in two directions. I long to have a space to pray, but I also long to leap up and wash the dishes. If I do succumb to the lure of the kitchen (which is never so strong at other times) it is fatal. As soon as I've finished washing the last spoon, you can guarantee that the doorbell will ring and my chance for a quiet time with God will be lost altogether.

It is so easy to be like the men in the parable and make excuses to miss the banquet (Luke 14).

★ ★ ★ ★ ★

When you pray, go into your room and shut the door and pray to your Father who is in secret. (Matthew 6:6)

8. But I waste the prayer-time once I've got it!

The essential act of prayer is to stand unprotected before God. What will God do? He will take possession of us. — Wendy Mary Beckett.

An irritating thing about prayer times is that we so often seem to waste them. We manage to set aside twenty minutes or so for prayer, but our mind flits around like an agitated bluebottle. However hard we try to focus our attention on God, our thoughts rattle on, both about important concerns and about trivial things. At the end of our precious few minutes alone with God we feel thoroughly disgruntled, as if we have thrown away the whole time.

There is a story that the Devil was once watching someone struggling unsuccessfully to concentrate on his prayer. The Devil remarked gleefully to God: 'That wasn't much good, was it!' But God replied: 'Nonsense! He did it for me.'

Obviously this is no excuse for being slapdash with God. We must still try to pray as well as we can. But God does understand our genuine desire to love Him, even if we make a mess of prayer times. He sees into our hearts and knows our motives.

Even the greatest saints have had problems with distraction. The main thing is not to despair or give in. That *would* be a victory for the Devil. So what do we do about the infuriating jangle in our chatter-box brains?

When there is a lot on our mind, it is probably best to start off talking to God about it, rather than gritting our teeth in an enforced silence straight away. We can hold each concern before God like an offering in our hands. It may be something we are pleased or worried about, or just our plans for the day. Then it helps to picture that we are handing all these things over to God, as if to say, 'Now You hold them in *Your* hands for a bit, so that I can quieten down and listen, and simply be with You'.

The trouble is that we keep taking things back again, out of God's hands and into our own. We also wander off in all directions until we suddenly realise what has happened. Then we have to keep giving our preoccupations back to Him, over and over again if necessary.

There is another important point. Usually it is right to let go of our distractions, so that we can gently return to the stillness with God. But occasionally the recurring thought is itself something we should be praying about. In that case we must pitch our tent in the place to which we have wandered. God wants us there for the moment.

But how do we distinguish between these two sorts of distraction? There is no easy formula to answer this question from the outside. We can only find out for ourselves by perservering. People who pray a great deal say that it becomes clear in time which of our distractions should be turned into prayers.

★   ★   ★   ★   ★

'I've got a chance to be quiet now ... I'm very tired, Lord. Thank you that the staff meeting wasn't as bad as I expected ... I'm sorry I was so irritable this afternoon ... Please be with the fourth and fifth forms doing their exams this week ...

'... I wonder how next term's timetable is going to work out; maybe I'll be doing more geography with the juniors ... That was a good programme we watched on TV last night ... There's another episode on Monday, but Sally will miss it ...

'... I hope Tom doesn't have so many discipline problems next year ... I pray for him, Lord ...

'... I put all the plans for next term into Your hands ...

'... Bible passage for today: Thomas sees Jesus, after doubting that He was risen, and says, 'My Lord and my God' ...

'... Jesus, I am Yours; You are my lord and my God ...

'... I wouldn't mind doing political studies with the fourth years next term ... Sorry, Lord! I do want to be with You ...

'... Jesus, my Lord and my God; do what You want with me ...

'... Lord ...'

★   ★   ★   ★   ★

You shall love the Lord your God with all your heart, and with all your soul, and with all your might. (Deut 6:5).

As a hart longs for flowing streams, so longs my soul for Thee, O God. (Psalm 42:1).

9. Into silence

The language that God best hears is the silent language of
love. — St John of the Cross.

There are many ways of coming to the stillness of prayer, and no single
method is the absolute and only path. It is God's work, anyway, so we
could not possibly dictate how He is to work in any of us. All we are
doing is learning to open ourselves up to Him, setting the scene; then
we hand over to God.

This is holy ground! It seems presumptuous to write about it at all.
All we can do is explore some of the ways in which God has drawn
countless people towards Himself.

A short word or phrase which has been our staunch ally through the
day (see Section 6) can lead us into peaceful communion with God
when we repeat it during a quiet time. Gradually we realise that as well
as loving God, we are being loved by Him. It is like sun-bathing: we
face the light and absorb it in a still act of surrender. We have to stop
thinking about what we are doing, and just get on and *do* it. The heart
of contemplative prayer is standing completely exposed and empty
before God. As we gently let go of our rattling thoughts we move into
the sort of loving which does not need words. We find ourselves in
tune with the silence at the heart of all creation.

Sometimes we only open up to God fully in the last few moments of
a prayer time. This is exasperating. Just as we are becoming quiet with
Him, we have to stop and go to work or cook a meal. Yet it doesn't
matter that our mind was wandering all over the place two minutes
ago. Everything that matters is here: our total surrender and love of
God in *this* moment. The value of prayer cannot be measured in
minutes and seconds. There is no point in regretting what *might* have
been in the earlier parts of a prayer time, or trying to recapture what we
should have been doing then. It is *now* that we are loving God. Even if

it is just for a few moments, heaven and earth have become one. That is something of eternal value.

★ ★ ★ ★ ★

There are times in ordinary life when words are totally inadequate. When someone faces intense grief there is nothing you can say, because their emotion goes beyond our everyday concepts and thoughts. Great happiness can also reduce us to silence. I remember being speechless with joy when each of my babies was first put into my arms.

It is a sign of a good friendship if you can be together without carrying on a non-stop conversation. We are all familiar with the opposite situation, when you are introduced to someone at a party and struggle to keep the conversation going with a mutual lack of interest. Close friends going for a walk or spending a day together do not have to talk all the time; they can simply enjoy being with each other. It is a moving experience to be with an elderly couple who have been happily married for years. Their quiet contentment as they sit together says more than an anthology of love poetry.

The same applies in our relationship with God. The Pharisees poured out their 'many words' to Him, thinking that there was some virtue in their verbal clutter. Of course we often do need to use words in prayer. But our friendship with God will not deepen much if we can never stop talking when we are with Him. When we manage to be still and open and ready to listen, we give God space to work in us in ways we never imagined.

★ ★ ★ ★ ★

Be still and know that I am God. (Psalm 46:10)

10. When prayer is a blank

The hard times are not obstacles to the growth of love,
although they will constantly seem to be such when we are
young. Rather they are a necessary part of the experience by
which real love comes to be. — Thomas H. Green.

At last we begin to find a deep inner stillness. Prayer becomes a source of joy, and we feel flooded with the incomparable peace of God. Then — crash! Our times of silence become dry and tedious and we lose the sense of God's presence. This fills us with alarm and disappointment. Are we going backwards? What has happened to that wonderful experience of serenity and grace? It is particularly discouraging if this happens when we had made a great effort to take a space for prayer in a busy day. 'What a waste,' we say to ourselves. 'What has gone wrong?'

It helps to know that nearly everyone who takes contemplative prayer seriously faces patches of spiritual dryness. The experience is described in all the great books on prayer.

The vital thing is that God has not abandoned us, even though we cannot feel His closeness as we did. Don't panic! God is leading us through a new phase in our friendship with Him, so that we will learn to want *Him* and not the pleasant experience of prayer for its own sake.

The purpose of prayer is not to give us a nice, cosy feeling. We all know that in theory. But in practice we hate it when our own sense of God's love suddenly disappears. 'Look here, Lord! Where do You think You've gone? Is this all the thanks I get for trying to love You?'

Perhaps we were hankering after times of prayer for the wrong reasons. If we are overworked and harassed, it is tempting to look forward to quiet times so much that the rest of life becomes almost a nuisance to be endured between those havens of holiness. Joy and exhilaration are often the results of prayer, but never the aim. It is not really important how we happen to feel when we pray. Periods of dryness are an opportunity to purify our love of God, and to grow in trust. We need to ask ourselves the hard question: 'What *do* I want? Do I long to love God for His own sake alone?'

Fortunately God's infinite mercy is there to bring us through. We just have to hang on. He is closer than we think.

★ ★ ★ ★ ★

'Father, for better or for worse, in sickness and in health, in light and in darkness, I give myself to You.'

★ ★ ★ ★ ★

Even though I walk through the valley of the shadow of death, I fear no evil; For thou art with me; thy rod and thy staff, they comfort me. (Psalm 23:4)

11. Inner silence all the time

To keep my mind free from confusion in order that my
liberty may be always at the disposal of His will; to entertain
silence in my heart and listen for the voice of God . . .
— Thomas Merton.

What is the point of being peaceful with God at prayer times when the
rest of life seethes with activity and noise? I seem to be two people —
the person who finds God in the stillness and the person who clatters
and hurries through the rest of the day. How can I hold the two sides of
myself together? This is the heartfelt cry of many of us who have felt
drawn towards a comtemplative silence with God while still living a
busy and sometimes chaotic life.

But silent prayer does not have to be limited to quiet times. This is
the crucial fact which keeps us sane. The stillness of God's love can
spill over into the whole of life, even the most unlikely bits, if we can
learn to receive it. There is nothing to stop us returning to our still
centre of prayer at any moment. We can do it when we are going to
work, washing up, or anything else.

To be inwardly quiet while doing something else, it helps to relax
the back of the throat and neck, especially if we are harassed or tired.
Slowly repeating a 'word friend' (see Section 6) can bring us out of
mental restlessness into a peaceful frame of mind. Bit by bit, we let go
of the stream of chatter flowing through our brain, so that we become
open and listen to God while we carry on our day's work. To do this
requires practice. We have to be patient with ourselves because we
keep going back to the rattling thoughts.

We easily lose heart. 'It's all right for the holy people,' we say, 'But
my mind darts around all the time and I am constantly distracted. I
could never manage the inner stillness you speak of.' Yet we all have

the same problem, from monks in mountain caves to parents of lively children. Most of us lose our inner silence only a few moments after finding it. That doesn't matter. The only way to grow is to persevere, and to turn gently back and back to the still point of communion with God. If we keep trying, we are not failing. We are travelling, taking the early steps in an adventure with God which lasts a lifetime — and beyond.

There is another problem. If we can pray all the time, why have periods set apart for prayer at all? We discover the answer to this question when we experiment for ourselves. If we try to be centred in stillness without bothering to take the chances we have for longer prayer times, the source of peace welling up inside us may run dry. The more we pray in the silence of times set aside for God alone, the more naturally we find inner quietness while busy working.

★　★　★　★　★

There is a church on a traffic island in the middle of a big city. It is one of the most peaceful places you can go to. Its stillness does not lie in the absence of noise; cars and buses screech around it all day. You find quietness there because people have prayed in that church for years, and God has come to meet them when they have stopped to receive Him there.

You don't have to be in a cool and prayerful building to find stillness with God, though it is a great help. You can create what has been called an 'interior cell' or 'portable chapel' of your own. The church in the traffic is a twentieth-century symbol of the same thing.

★　★　★　★　★

'And a great storm of wind arose, and the waves beat into the boat, so that the boat was already filling. But Jesus was in the stern, asleep on the cushion; and they woke Him and said to Him, 'Teacher, do you not care if we perish?'

'And He awoke and rebuked the wind, and said to the sea, 'Peace! Be still!' And the wind ceased, and there was a great calm.' (Mark 4: 37-39)

12. How many people am I?

At the still point of the turning world. Neither flesh nor
fleshless; Neither from nor towards; at the still point, there
the dance is . . . — T. S. Eliot.

Most of us live a fragmented existence, jerking from one role to
another. We are parents one minute and office workers the next; we are
marriage partners at this moment and members of committees or
sports clubs at another. The person in us who prays often feels poles
apart from the person who runs a home and goes to work.

Yet inward stillness holds us together and is like a hidden stream
running through everything we do. Even though we often forget all
about it, our still centre is always there to come back to, whatever
different aspects of our personality happen to be uppermost at the
time.

When we are quiet with God, we are most truly ourselves. We are
not wearing this hat or that hat, nor are we putting on any of the faces
or facades we show to the world. We are simply ourselves. So by
allowing that stillness with God to permeate all our activities, we
become less broken up into separate bits. We begin to discover who we
are: somebody who is forgiven and loved by God, all the time.

★   ★   ★   ★   ★

I once helped to organise a meeting at which the Russian Orthodox
Archbishop Anthony Bloom was speaking. He is a doctor as well as a
priest. While he was walking to the meeting place, he stopped to help a
lady who had collapsed in the road. This meant that he arrived to speak
to us a few minutes late. Those of us who organised the event were
flapping around like a lot of agitated hens, but Archbishop Anthony
remained completely calm.

The secret of his utter tranquility was his peaceful communion with God, which was unbroken through all the hurry and interruption of that evening. The priest and the doctor and the preacher in him were all one, because each of those aspects of his life was based on a quiet prayerfulness underneath.

★   ★   ★   ★   ★

For God alone my soul waits in silence,
   for my hope is from Him.
He only is my rock and my salvation,
   my fortress; I shall not be shaken.
                    (Psalm 62:5-6)

13. Many kinds of wilderness

In all things, inner silence. Even when Christ Jesus seems absent, He is always beside you. In all things, remain in His presence. That is what matters most. At this source you can draw that irreplaceable trust in God. — Brother Roger.

You don't have to be a self-denying hermit or a monk in the Sahara to experience the wilderness-with-God.

We all go through a wilderness experience at some time. We may be worried or unwell, surrounded by demanding people, or frustrated at work. Perhaps we have no job, or our home is full of tensions. Mothers of young children sometimes feel they will never shake themselves free from a swamp of domestic chaos. Older people can face a wilderness of loneliness, with a sense of not being needed or useful any more.

If we are asked to describe a wilderness, the picture which immediately comes to mind is of a barren, unattractive landscape with occasional rocks and scrub; a dangerous and unwelcoming place, where you feel helpless and lost. We always tend to see 'wilderness' in negative terms. But does it have to be so utterly void of peace or prayerfulness?

Jesus *chose* to go into the wilderness for a long period of prayer, clearly because He knew that He could be closer to God there than anywhere else. For two thousand years Christians have been drawn to encounter God in wild and lonely places. This great tradition of prayer in the desert has continued, from the Egyptian fathers of the fifth century, to Carlo Carretto in the present day.[1]

In the wilderness Christians have struggled, as Jesus did, with the powers of evil, and have exposed the depths of their soul to God. And that parched, comfortless environment has become the place where they have been touched by God's infinite love more deeply than ever before.

All this is not as remote from everyday life as it may seem. Our own particular wilderness can be transformed as well (even though we didn't choose to be here). Our depression, our doubt, our loneliness, can become the place where we too find God in a new and profound way. We need to stop for a moment and stand before God, empty and helpless, like a nomad reaching out to the vast desert sky. In the simplicity of that moment, something happens. God is there. Even if we cannot feel His presence, we can be absolutely certain that God is with us, because we are making space for Him.

A 'word friend' (see Section 6) is then a great help during the rest of the day, bringing us back to stillness with God over and over again.

Most of us are very bad at praying in this way. We are tempted to give up when we read about outstanding people like St Antony of Egypt, whose interior silence was so intense that his whole life was one constant prayer. Ordinary mortals like us don't manage to quieten our minds for long. Yet every fragment of time in which we make our wilderness a place of prayer is of infinite value. It is *wanting* to pray that matters most.

Obviously when life is hell we are in no state to think clearly about deserts or wildernesses or anything else. (The whole question of pain is looked at in a later section.) But in a less acute kind of trouble we can find that we are not in a spiritual dead end after all. We make the amazing discovery that our most unlikely and unpromising situation can become the heart of a new kind of praying, more powerful than we had ever known before. In our helplessness we rediscover that we are nothing and God is all. That is the essence of contemplative prayer.

★   ★   ★   ★   ★

Living alone is a wilderness experience for some people. Many solitary grandparents find it hard to adjust to not being needed by their family as they used to be. Although many single people value their independence, there are also those who long for the depth of a lifetime relationship with someone. Being alone is their wilderness.

It is also hard *never* to be alone. Being constantly surrounded by the demands and noise of other people can itself be another kind of spiritual wilderness.

There is not so very much difference between the barren rocks around the hermit and the difficult mundane situation we may face. In both cases *this* is where our prayer starts; this is where we have to reach out in total dependence on God, and where He comes to find us.

'Father, wherever You lead me, I will go. I depend on You; I trust You.'

★ ★ ★ ★ ★

Moses said to Joshua towards the end of the years in the wilderness: *Be strong and of good courage; for it is the Lord your God who goes with you ... He will not fail you or forsake you; do not fear or be dismayed.* (Deut 31:6, 8)

NOTES

1. Carlo Caretto's books include *Letters From the Desert* (Darton, Longman and Todd) and *Desert in the City* (Collins Fount).

Part two
The way we look at life

14. The gift of the present moment

A soul can be truly nourished, strengthened, purified, enriched and sanctified only by the divine plenitude of the present moment. What more do you want? Since all that is good is here, why seek it elsewhere? — Jean-Pierre de Caussade.

The present moment is all we have; we can only live and love *now*. The only place we can find God is where we are at this moment. Yet many of us find it incredibly hard to live fully in the present. There are all kinds of reasons for this.

Those whose lives are miserable tend to dwell on happier days of the past. They cannot find strength to cope with the present situation because all their mental and spiritual energy is being poured into their world of memories. So the past becomes idealised, an escape from the challenges needing to be faced now.

It is not only older people who can make this mistake. When any of us falls in love, we are just as bad! We daydream so much about last night's date that we find it most difficult to concentrate on this morning's work.

Living too much in the future is another hazard. If we know that we will soon be moving to a job elsewhere, we easily lose interest in the situation where we are now working. Discontentment also makes us dwell on the future: 'When I leave here,' we say, or, 'When I retire,' or 'When we have a better house, *then* everything will be all right.' By assuming that the next phase in our life is bound to be marvellous, we can make ourselves increasingly grumpy about present circumstances.

Sometimes the promotion mentality takes over. 'Nothing we do is of value in itself; work is useful only as a means of getting on in the world.' So we just mark time in our present employment. We study for examinations, not out of interest or enjoyment in what we are learning, but simply to get on, get in, and get up.

We risk throwing away great chunks of our lives in this way. We are not living fully at all, but just existing here while our hearts are somewhere else.

This restlessness makes our relationship with God difficult because in prayer we draw all the various bits of ourselves together before Him. It is not easy to open our whole selves up to God in the stillness if parts of our concern and interest are in one place and parts in another. Nor will we find inward quietness in the middle of a day's work unless we are totally given to the present moment and ready to meet God there.

★   ★   ★   ★   ★

When our children are drawing pictures or riding bicycles or making models, we often think, 'Ah, good, that will help their schoolwork, or stretch their muscles, or develop their creative skills for the future.' But for the children themselves these are valuable activities in their own right. It is exciting to build a town out of blocks or play a difficult tune in the piano book, not because it will pave the way for a successful career but because it is fun. They are right. In their ability to be absorbed in the present moment, children have much to teach us about the contemplative way.

★   ★   ★   ★   ★

St Paul wrote: *You know what hour it is, how it is full time now for you to wake from sleep. For salvation is nearer to us now than when we first believed; the night is far gone, the day is at hand.* (Romans 13:11-12)

15. Making space

Cultivate freedom of spirit, spaciousness of mind: live in peace, boldly and with tranquility. — Abbé de Tourville.

Being busy is another obstacle to living fully in the present. Plans tumble over each other in our minds as we rush from job to job. We mutter restlessly to ourselves: 'If he hadn't come into the office, I would have finished this typing by now'; 'If the children want any more help with their homework I'll never get down to reading the paper'; 'After I've decorated this room I'll paper the hall, and then I'll start upstairs and then ...'

The task we are doing at that moment is spoiled because our mind is not fully on it. We become tense and irritable, 'distracted from distraction by distraction' like the harassed, time-racked commuters in T. S. Eliot's *Four Quartets*[1].

We have to let go of other concerns so that we can concentrate our whole self on the work we are doing now. If we have lots to do, it can help to write a list of all our jobs. Then we know that we will not forget anything, so there is no need to clutter up our mind with them any more.

Many people like to listen to music while doing mechanical jobs. This does not necessarily stop us living in the present, because we can still be wholly receptive to the music while our hands do something else. But if we start thinking about all the other things we need to do, our listening is spoilt. When the record comes to an end, we realise that we were not really listening at all.

Sometimes we convince ourselves that we will start living fully again once we have completed this, this and this. But that is an illusion, because we have never finally finished. As soon as we have done one set of jobs there will always be a fresh batch of uncompleted tasks. Weeds grow, letters need answering, clothes get dirty; life moves on, and the world will not stand still to allow us to catch up.

Maybe we have too much on our plate. If we have taken on too many commitments, we end up fulfilling none of them properly. In order to make space for the right things, we may have to do some ruthless pruning.

But what is so important about living in the present? Why should we bother to make space at all? It is so that we can enjoy life more, give more to life, and come to know God more deeply. *Now* is sacred, because this is the point where God is to be encountered; not next week but here, in the middle of all our work and contacts with other people. When we have made space for whatever is happening around us, we can be centred in the stillness of God. That is what is meant by living contemplatively.

★   ★   ★   ★   ★

'Yes, but there is so much to do!' We have to make an act of faith and trust the timing of things to God. After all, it is He who gives us our life and the work we have to do, as well as the means to do it. If He gives the material, won't He also provide the opportunity?

The way to listen to God's timing rather than our own frantic schedule is to be inwardly still instead of rushing round and only living on the surface of life. We may find a sense of the rightness of what we are doing at *this* moment, when we stop trying to do too many things at once. Then we become more sensitive to what might be called the rhythm of things.

Our still centre of prayer is like a bulb or rhizome, lying hidden beneath all our activity. If we live contemplatively, everything we do springs from this life source. Just as leaves and flowers fade and die off while the rhizome remains, so our activity is a passing and secondary thing compared to 'living in the kingdom' (as Meister Eckhardt calls it) in our deepest being, all the time.

An Exercise with a Marble

Try this! If you have lots to do in a short time, try an exercise with a marble.

Before you rush to do the next job, STOP, just for a moment. (This seems daft because it cuts down the time you have even more. But try it.) Your mind is probably buzzing with all that needs doing, like a marble rolling round a large wooden bowl. Stop and picture that marble going round and round, gradually coming to the centre of the bowl, and stopping there, remaining quite still. Let your own mind, like the marble, slow down and stop at this central point, which is where you are, here and now. You are now ready to do the job with the whole of yourself and not just a harassed part of your mind (while the rest of your thoughts were racing round uncontrollably). Your mind is quiet, and you can concentrate fully on the task in hand. Now get to work!

If you wish, you can decide which job you will do after this one. But plan no further ahead than that. Don't let the marble start rolling round again.

The marble method doesn't suit everyone. But we can all find our own way of pulling ourselves together into one place.

★   ★   ★   ★   ★

To another Jesus said, 'Follow me.' But he said, 'Lord, let me first go and bury my father.' But He said to him, 'Leave the dead to bury their own dead; but as for you, go and proclaim the kingdom of God.'

Another said, 'I will follow you, Lord; but let me first say farewell to those at my home.' Jesus said to him, 'No one who puts his hand to the plough and looks back is fit for the kingdom of God.' (Luke 9:59-62)

NOTES

1. 'Burnt Norton' 1.101.

16. Hurry can hurt, space can heal

Healing is as wide as creation and is the motive force within
it. ... Too often we tend to think of physical healing only,
but the purpose of our Creator for us is infinitely greater. He
has unleashed a power that must heal totally and bring us
into that spaciousness of health. — Bishop Morris
Maddocks.

Have peace in your heart, and thousands around you will be
healed. — St Seraphim of Sarov.

Making space for people is a healing activity. We help others more
than we realise in those rare moments when we manage to give them
our whole attention. By living contemplatively in the present moment,
we enable God's energy of love and healing to work through us.

The opposite is also true. It can be positively harmful to our families
and friends if we are forever busy and distracted.

Giving people time helps them to grow and blossom; always being
in a hurry is a way of squashing people. So we are all instruments of
hurting or healing in the world whether we like it or not.

Hurry can hurt

A civil servant takes early retirement, but his wife carries on working
in a local library. The husband enjoys gardening but finds it does not
fill his time. The sudden emptiness of his life leads to depression and
he longs to talk about it to his wife. But she is so preoccupied with
getting the meals and going to Women's Institute meetings that she
never stops to listen properly. In the end he stops trying to share
anything with her and sinks into a deeper lethargy of disappointment
and frustration. Things are going wrong in that marriage largely
because his wife is so preoccupied with hurrying from one activity to
another.

Hurry can hurt, even in simple things like not reading a letter properly, or gobbling down a meal which has taken hours to cook. Many car crashes are caused by unnecessary haste; and many hearts are wounded because people are in too much of a hurry to notice or say Thank you.

Space can heal

When my children are tired and tense after a day at school, they will often calm down and be themselves again if I manage to forget about other concerns and concentrate on simply being with them. Something peaceful happens because space has been made for a power other than myself to work.

It takes time to listen to the agonies of a son or daughter worried about their maths, or unable to keep up in swimming lessons. But by giving them our whole attention we can help them to find confidence.

When anybody is unhappy they need someone who will listen attentively to them. Just being there so that people can pour out their troubles is itself a healing action. The more we are able to be inwardly still and prayerful ourselves, the more God can use us as channels of His loving power, sometimes in remarkable ways.

★ ★ ★ ★ ★

Jesus came to a village where a woman named Martha welcomed Him in her home. She had a sister named Mary, who sat down at the feet of the Lord and listened to His teaching. Martha was upset over all the work she had to do, so she came and said, 'Lord, don't you care that my sister has left me to do all the work by myself? Tell her to come and help me!'

The Lord answered her, 'Martha, Martha! You are worried and troubled over so many things, but just one is needed. Mary has chosen the right thing, and it will not be taken away from her.' (Luke 10:38-42. Good News Bible)

17. Interruptions

A condition of complete simplicity, costing not less than
everything. — T. S. Eliot.

It is a luxury to be able to complete one job before starting the next. All our good intentions to give ourselves totally to the task in hand can be shattered by interruptions. Sometimes the first interruption is in turn interrupted by something else, so that we entirely lose the thread of where we were and what we were trying to do. Surrounded by unfinished tasks, we feel as if we are running up an escalator which is going downwards. It is a struggle to hang on to inward peacefulness in the frustration of seeing all our plans blown out of the window. At such moments my prayer is, 'Lord, help me to find Your wholeness in the middle of incompleteness.'

We have to find a way of prayerful acceptance as each interruption comes. We must let go of what we were doing, leaving it firmly in God's hands for the moment, so that we are free to turn our whole attention to the person who has come into the office, or the child who has lost his teddy, or the caller on the telephone. By giving ourselves to the need in front of us, we can regain our inner surrender and stillness and respond as if there were nobody else and nothing else at that moment. In our rising frustration we have to entrust to God the jobs we haven't even started yet, as well as the unfinished ones. This is an act of faith. If we have given ourselves to God in everything, we can trust Him to see us through everything.

★ ★ ★ ★ ★

'Just back from holiday — piles of letters to answer and papers to read — trying to finish unpacking — "Mummy, can we do some painting?" — "Please would you mend the chain on my bike?" —

"Where's my hairbrush?" — "Mummy, my knitting's in a knot"...

'... Just changing the baby when a voice from downstairs calls, "I've fallen over in the nettles" — searching frantically for the soothing-cream when the doorbell goes...

'... It's nearly tea time and we haven't enough bread — we must put on wellies to go to the shop because it is raining hard — while hunting for those the telephone rings — during that phone call the toddler has gone into the muddy back garden in his socks ...'

This harassed mother has to find what might be called a 'vertical' wholeness in the middle of the 'horizontal' incompleteness around her. Wholeness, for her, is to be found in the way she looks at her children's paintings, answers their questions and picks them up when they fall over. Wholeness lies in trying to love and remain Christ-centred in the present moment; and the present moment is very often an interruption.

★　★　★　★　★

There were so many people coming and going that Jesus and His disciples didn't even have time to eat. So He said to them, 'Let us go off by ourselves to some place where we will be alone and you can rest for a while.' So they started out in a boat by themselves for a lonely place.

Many people, however, saw them leave, and knew at once who they were; so they went from all the towns and ran ahead by land and arrived at the place ahead of Jesus and His disciples. When Jesus got out of the boat, He saw this large crowd, and His heart was filled with pity for them, because they were like sheep without a shepherd. So He began to teach them many things. (Mark 6:31-34. Good News Bible)

18. What is going on underneath?

> If we knew how to look at life through God's eyes, all life
> would become a sign. If we knew how to listen to God, all
> life would become prayer. — Michel Quoist.

If we try to live contemplatively, we will learn to stand still and look beneath the surface of external events. A brief glance at a painting in a gallery will tell us that the artist has put coloured chemicals onto a piece of canvas of a certain size. But to see the picture properly we must take time to stop and look, emptying our own mind and losing ourselves in all that the artist is expressing.

You don't necessarily have to be a religious person to see the deeper realities of life. But the prayer of contemplation sharpens our capacity to be open and aware of God and His world, so that we become more sensitive to what is happening underneath.

When a couple have an argument about a kitchen gadget, the problem is almost certainly concerned with their relationship and not primarily about methods of cooking. If a child misbehaves he or she may be saying, 'Look at me, I want some attention.' There are some vandals who cause trouble out of a sense of futility and a wish for the excitement of breaking things up. But others are giving vent to a deep frustration: 'I can make my mark even if I can't get work; I am just as strong as you are; take notice of me, someone.' Outward appearances can be deceptive until we are able to discern what is going on inside people and what they are really saying when they do things.

Two identical boxes of chocolates might be given as presents. One could be from a possessive person who wants to tighten their grip on someone by making them grateful. The other box could be simply a gift from a kind friend. The chocolates may look the same, but they are essentially different when their real significance is seen.

If we are as open to life as we try to be towards God in prayer, we will increasingly see through the exterior of things to the interior truth beneath. All of life is a kind of parable. Everything we do is an outward expression of our inner attitude. The way I am sitting conveys my state of mind: you can tell if I am depressed, alert or peaceful by whether I am slumped, upright or relaxed in my chair.

As Christians we seek to make all we do a concrete sign of our inward Yes to Christ. This is living sacramentally. In a sense the whole of Jesus's life was a sign, holding heaven and earth together. He focussed the extra-ordinary gift of Himself in the most ordinary elements of bread and wine. No other meal has ever had such sublime significance for those with eyes to see.

*   *   *   *   *

The people with the deepest insight are those who are constantly turned towards Jesus in prayer. This is why Mother Theresa sees Christ in the destitute and sore-ridden people she serves. This is why she sees so clearly the horror of what we are doing in our automatic abortion mentality, and the blasphemy of weapons which could totally destroy God's world.

Our comparatively mundane lives can also take on a profound significance if we know how to look. Eating a slice of bread while listening to a radio report about a famine can be a moment of searching penitence as well as thanksgiving. The way we eat at any time conveys our inward attitude to the gift of food, which has been called 'divine love made edible'. Bread is so easy to buy hurriedly from the shops that we hardly ever pause to appreciate the growth of wheat and the processes of farming and baking which it represents.

Vision makes us vulnerable. The more we see the more we feel involved in the vital issues around us. This can lead to pain, not only as we realise our own sinfulness and the sin of the world but also because we will face criticism, as Jesus Himself and all the great prophets have done. Figures like William Wilberforce, Martin Luther King, and Bishop David Sheppard in our own time are Christians who have seen and exposed the reality underneath cruel attitudes and prejudices in society and suffered misunderstanding and hostility as a result. We too may be hurt if we speak out about what we see happening under the surface of our own community. It would be much easier to stay in a blind and cosy cocoon, unseeing, uncaring, uninvolved. But to do that is to die.

★ ★ ★ ★ ★

Then the disciples came and said to Jesus, 'Why do you speak to them in parables?' And He answered them, 'To you it has been given to know the secrets of the kingdom of heaven, but to them it has not been given. This is why I speak to them in parables, because seeing they do not see, and hearing they do not hear, nor do they understand . . . lest they should perceive with their eyes and hear with their ears, and understand with their heart, and turn for me to heal them.' (Matt 13:10-15)

19. Does it really matter?

In the evening of life we shall be judged on love. — St John of the Cross.

The contemplative way of looking beneath the surface of life gives us a new perspective: some things don't seem to matter so much now, while others become more important. We see that efficiency is not always the first priority in a human situation; sometimes understanding and kindness have to take precedence. Activities do not need to be useful in order to be valuable. Being a hostess is far more than making beds and cooking special meals: what matters most is the peaceful welcome that enables people to relax and be themselves.

Jesus was constantly clashing with the Pharisees over this question of priorities. They idolised their external regulations, paying detailed attention to washing and eating rituals and a whole range of pernickity religious observances. Yet they overlooked the hidden essentials of gentleness and love (Mark 7 and Matt 23). We can become like the Pharisees without realising it when we fuss over inessentials and hurt other people in the process. The stillness of prayer should help to stop us being restless about things that are not of prime importance, and to open ourselves up to share Christ's wider vision of what matters in life.

★ ★ ★ ★ ★

Your children prepare the tea on a day when you are not feeling well. All the wrong china appears on the table, and a strange assortment of cutlery. Does this matter enough for you to point it out? How will the children feel if you do?

A well paid man never takes his wife out for a meal on the grounds that it is too expensive; a mother refuses to take her children to the pantomime for the same reason. By doing this they are really saying: 'Saving money is more important to me than giving you a treat.'

A building society employee moves to work with a different society. On the first day there he unwittingly files some papers in the wrong cabinet. His superior makes a scene about this in front of the customers and other staff so that he feels humiliated. Concern to keep everything exactly in order matters more to that man than the feelings of the junior clerk.

You come home to find the living room full of children surrounded by scraps of paper, glitter and paint. How do you look at the scene? Do you see it as an irritating mess that should be cleared up instantly? Or do you see it as a group of contented children producing an important frieze? What matters most to you — their activity or a spotless house?

★　★　★　★　★

Now when Jesus was at Bethany in the house of Simon the leper, a woman came up to Him with an alabaster flask of very expensive ointment, and she poured it on His head as He sat at table.

But when the disciples saw it, they were indignant, saying, 'Why this waste? For this ointment might have been sold for a large sum, and given to the poor.'

But Jesus said to them, 'Why do you trouble the woman? For she has done a beautiful thing to me : . .

. . . For you always have the poor with you, but you will not always have me. In pouring this ointment on my body she has done it to prepare me for burial. (Matt 26:6-12)

20. A child's eye view

What is serious to man is often very trivial in the sight of God. What in God might appear to us as 'play' is, perhaps, what He Himself takes most seriously. — Thomas Merton.

Children often get things right. Jesus knew this, and He told us to be like little children ourselves.

Children often see the goodness in things because they have not yet learned to be cynical. They make friends naturally with children of another colour, and only discover racial prejudice later. The great cricketer Sir Leary Constantine tells how a small boy used to come and practise batting and bowling with him near his house in Lancashire. One day the boy came in tears: 'My dad says I mustn't play with you any more. It's not fair. Why didn't you tell me you're black?'

Children are not cluttered up with as many unnecessary concerns as adults. They know how to stop and look and be totally lost in something exciting like a ladybird or a model engine. They are natural contemplatives (as well as being incredibly noisy at times!). Finding again the simplicity of a child is not reverting to childishness; it is rediscovering a certain way of looking and trusting and receiving.

★   ★   ★   ★   ★

Last winter my son walked straight into the deepest patch of snow he could find at the side of the path in our local park. I retorted in a typically adult way, 'But you'll have to change your trousers when you get home.' He nodded in agreement and then carried on with the important business of enjoying the snow while it was there. He knew what mattered at that moment better than I did.

There was a similar lesson to learn from my three-year-old, who loves to stand and watch the big library lorry coming out of its garage. However cold or miserable the weather, the moment is filled with magic for him as the great blue giant emerges. Every time I have to struggle with my impatience and tell myself, 'Of course he's right. Why rush home when there is something so special to do?' One day the driver invited my son to look at the books in the back of the lorry. He was shy at first; but when he ventured in, his happiness was complete. And to think we could have missed that delight for the sake of five-minutes' more housework!

As adults we are aware of the complexities of the world economy and the difficulties involved in sending aid to developing countries. But on seeing starving families on the television news, my six-year-old daughter asked, 'Why can't we give them half our food, so that we're hungry one day and they're hungry the next?'

Children are never perfect plaster cherubs. (The next minute we were all arguing about who had the biggest piece of chocolate.) But they do nevertheless have that clear and uncluttered vision of life which makes them ask the right questions.

★　★　★　★　★

Whoever does not receive the kingdom of God like a child shall not enter it. (Luke 18:17)

Part three
Pain and failure

21. God is not a Super Rescue Service

He said not, 'Thou shalt not be troubled, thou shalt not be travailed, thou shalt not be distressed'; but He said, 'Thou shalt not be overcome'. — Mother Julian of Norwich.

Whether we like it or not, pain is part of the whole fabric of life. To escape suffering completely, we would have to live in some sort of sterilised and cushioned modules, with no risk of infection or accident. If there were no trouble, pain or difficulty in life, there would be no courage, patience, forgiveness or compassion either. We would never learn from our mistakes or grow through struggles and hard challenges. Goodness would just be the automatic response of puppet-people, because the freedom to choose good or evil would not be allowed. The more we try to imagine a painless and flawless world, the more impossible it becomes. Difficulty and suffering are an inescapable part of the mystery of being alive.

This does not make suffering any easier to bear. We still protest and fight against pain when it comes our way. We also complain about how unfair it all seems. If someone who is known to be a Christian faces illness or any other kind of hardship, people often say, 'Why did God let it happen to him if he's a believer?' We sometimes reduce God to a petty wonder worker who will intervene to protect His favourites from trouble. Some religious books come dangerously near to making God into a convenience, a Heavenly Rescue Service to be summoned when it suits us — as long as we have enough faith.

This approach to God is a far cry from the call of Jesus to give our all, take up our cross and follow Him. Discipleship can let us in for more suffering, not less.

Throughout the Bible, men of God have served Him at enormous cost to themselves. Elijah had to flee for his life after standing up against the idolatrous queen Jezebel. Jeremiah was thrown into a muddy well because the word of God which he felt he had to proclaim was so unpopular.

It is fascinating to trace how biblical writers gradually came to terms with the question of pain and suffering. Many earlier Old Testament traditions held the simple belief that good behaviour brings good fortune and vice versa: 'If you obey the commandments of the Lord your God, the Lord will make you abound in prosperity; ... but if you will not obey the voice of the Lord, then all these curses shall come upon you ...' (Deut 28). But as Israel's understanding of God matured over the centuries, they began to ask the agonising question, 'Why do the wicked prosper?' (Jem 12:1). This searching reached a climax in the writings about Job, the innocent lover of God, who faced terrible suffering and ill fortune, and whose friends wrongly assumed that he must have sinned.

The greatest understanding of suffering in Old Testament times came when the Jews faced the humiliation of exile in Babylon. In the 500s BC the prophet Second Isaiah had the sublime vision of God's servant who was wounded and rejected for the sake of others (especially Is Chapter 53). This of course foreshadowed the life and death of Jesus, in whom God Himself suffered and reconciled the world to Himself.

In the New Testament it was rejection, mockery, whipping and crucifixion that Jesus had to face. But by coming through the horror of the cross undefeated, He turned suffering and evil upside down.

We cannot expect to go through life avoiding pain, any more than Jesus did. But the tremendous fact at the centre of our Christian faith is that God works through suffering to bring new life, healing, and a deepening of prayer.

* * * * *

If somebody steals some clothes off my washing line while I am indoors baking for a church cake stall, or if the tool bag is taken from my car while I am decorating an old lady's house, I feel like shaking my fist and saying, 'Now, look here, Lord! I'm doing my bit ... why should this happen to *me* of all people?' But why shouldn't it? Do I deserve to be more comfortable and secure than millions of other people in the world? Why should I be the lucky one?

Suffering is a mystery, and its distribution is certainly not based on merit or desert. (If it were, we'd all be permanently miserable anyway.) Jesus never promised us easy dodges from the hard things. What He does give, however, is the strength and the love to cope with pain in His way.

★   ★   ★   ★   ★

If any man would come after me, let him deny himself and take up his cross daily and follow me. For whoever would save his life will lose it; and whoever loses his life for my sake, he will save it. (Luke 9:23-24)

22. Pain is part of loving

*Love anything and your heart will certainly be wrung and
possibly broken. If you want to make sure of keeping it
intact you must give your heart to no one. — C. S. Lewis.*

If we wish for a painless world we are wishing away love as well. It is
because we love our families that we go through agony when they are
miserable. If we didn't care about our children, it wouldn't bother us
much when their class mates picked on them, or when they couldn't
find a job. It is terrible to see anyone we love being hurt or broken by
a painful experience. 'Com-passion' means, literally, 'suffering with'
someone. Love is costly.

Another reason why we are vulnerable when we love is that we are
placing a bit of ourselves and our happiness in someone else's hands.
They might not be fond of us in return; we cannot force them to love
us. We could easily be deeply hurt, and it is much safer not to love at
all!

Love can lead to suffering in other ways, too, as Jesus's life bears
out. Eating with Matthew the tax-collector's disreputable friends was
an act of love: Jesus had to endure the jealousy and criticism of the
Pharisees as a result. When He healed on the Sabbath it was because
love mattered to Him more than dry legalism; this attracted even
more hatred against Himself.

In the end Jesus's shattering combination of truth and love was too
much for us, the human race, to bear, so we crucified Him. Even
more shattering is the fact that He asks us to go the same way.

★   ★   ★   ★   ★

Your teenage son joins a group of lads who walk round the town
breaking things up. You know that he is not basically violent or cruel,
and you go on believing in him in spite of what has happened. When

you walk along the street, some neighbours look away; one person makes a cutting remark suggesting that you have failed as a parent. At that moment you are sharing your son's pain, taking much of the blame onto yourself. It is because of your love that you suffer a great deal for your son, bearing with him the consequences of what he has done.

★　★　★　★　★

Jesus said, 'This is my commandment, that you love one another as I have loved you. Greater love has no man than this, that a man lay down his life for his friends.' (John 15:12-13)

23. It hurts to let go

Obedience also demands of you
that you listen to the other person;
not only to what he is saying
but to what he is.
Then you will begin to live in such a way
that you neither crush nor dominate
nor entangle your brother
but help him to be himself
and lead him to freedom.
Christ was thus obedient
unto death. — 'Rule for a New Brother'

There is another way in which love involves pain: we have to let go of the person we love. As parents we must constantly decide when to hold on to our children and protect them, and when to let them find their independence. This conflict continues from the moment our toddlers take their first wobbly steps alone to the years when our teenagers stay out late and eventually leave home.

It is not only parents who are tempted to be possessive. When we think a lot of somebody, we instinctively want to hang on to them. A silly and unreasonable part of us wishes that the person we love would think more about us than about anyone else; we want to possess them for ourselves. But we cannot do this, and we mustn't try. To clutch them would be to destroy the essence of love, which is pouring out our heart while letting the other remain free. Surprisingly, when we do hold back we come much closer to the other person in the end.

All this is a glimpse of the mystery of God's own love for us. His act of creating mankind is a risk because He leaves us free to choose whether or not to love Him. He has not made us into robots or puppets; He lets us become generous or greedy, creative or destructive, compassionate or cruel. Being human means that God allows us to wound Him if we want to.

This is where prayer comes in. Our own experience of loving and letting go gives us a fragmentary glimpse of God's own suffering love, which is so great that it reduces us to silence and wonder.

★　★　★　★　★

Your closest friend falls in love and marries. Suddenly the special intimacy and confidence of your friendship changes, even though you are just as fond of each other. The adjustment is painful, because you have to stand back and let your friend go.

'You mustn't think that Dad and I would try to stop you going overseas because we wanted you close to us. You must go. It would be dishonest to say that we didn't mind your going — of course we do, because we shall miss you very much and worry about your safety. But we're also pleased and proud that you are needed there and that you want to go ...' (From a letter written to an 18-year-old going on Voluntary Service Overseas.)

★　★　★　★　★

The word of the Lord came to Hosea: 'When Israel was a child, I loved him ... The more I called them, the more they went from me; they kept sacrificing to the Baals, and burning incense to idols.

'Yet it was I who taught Ephraim to walk, I took them up in my arms; but they did not know that I healed them ...

'How can I give you up, O Ephraim! How can I hand you over, O Israel! My heart recoils within me, my compassion grows warm and tender; I will not execute my fierce anger, for I am God and not man, and I will not come to destroy.' (Hosea 11:1-3, 8-9)

24. When life is hell

Suffering is the great fertiliser of the spiritual life. —
Baudelaire.

Sometimes pain has nothing to do with loving or any other good cause
as far as we can see. It is just plain misery, making us want to scream
and kick against it. If someone has hurt us really badly, or if we are
shaken by bereavement or in great physical pain, the wave of suffering
completely engulfs us for a while. We find it almost impossible to be
open to other people because our own needs are so acute. We are not
aware of anything much except the pain itself.

The popular image of a Christian saint, heroically enduring
dreadful agonies with a sickly smile and all the right theological
answers at his fingertips, does nothing to help us. It only adds to our
despair to be told that as Christians we ought to be joyful in tribulation
and merry in misery. It seems impossible to pray as we usually do
because the suffering smothers everything else. From a wise and
experienced priest I have learned that all we can do is let the pain itself
become our prayer. We just have to hang on, perhaps literally to a
small wooden cross or in our minds to the name of Jesus. Although we
are not aware of it at the time, Jesus *is* there with us in the middle of it
all. He has gone through the agony, humiliation and utter rejection of
the cross, literally descending into hell. There is no darkness, evil or
pain beyond His reach.

To accept that fact in the middle of intense suffering is an act of
blind faith, because we probably don't feel close to Jesus at all. When
pain is at its fiercest, it takes all our strength to struggle on and cling to
our trust in God. But after the storm has eased a bit, and we are able to
reflect prayerfully about the experience, we may discover something
new. In a sense we had been reduced to nothing. All our defences had

collapsed, and other people saw us when we were down. We were overwhelmed, helpless, inadequate. From our own nothingness, we begin to realise that God is everything. In our weakness we see that we depend on Him totally. A new depth of surrender in prayer comes from this discovery.

This insight comes through pain and prayer, not cool, logical reasoning. Words alone cannot adequately convey such an experience. But if *you* have grown in dependence on God through suffering, you will know that it is true.

★　★　★　★　★

A couple were interviewed on TV three months after they had lost their baby through a rare illness. They said they had felt terrible anguish and helplessness when they were first told he would die. But, amazingly, they described his death as a 'homely moment' of 'stillness' and 'relief', now that the pain had gone from his face. The experience had, they said, shaken them out of their complacency and made them realise that they relied on God for everything. Their worship and faith had now become vital to them because they had had to go 'through and beyond the suffering' with God.

'We've grown through the tragedy,' the mother said. 'I think we're still learning. Maybe that's the resurrection — something we live every day, not just two thousand years ago ... Yes, we do hope to have another baby; but that's not under our control — we realise that now. It's given; all of life is given.'

★　★　★　★　★

Two bandits were crucified with Him, one on His right and the other on His left. The passers-by hurled abuse at Him: they wagged their heads and cried, 'Come down from the cross and save yourself, if you are indeed the Son of God.'

So too the chief priests with the lawyers and elders mocked at Him. 'He saved others,' they said, 'but He cannot save Himself.'

Even the bandits who were crucified with Him taunted Him in the same way.

Darkness fell over the whole land ... and Jesus cried aloud, 'Eli, Eli, lama sabachthani?' which means, 'My God, my God, why hast thou forsaken me?'

'... Then Jesus gave a loud cry and said, 'Father, into thy hands I commit my spirit;' and with these words He died.' (From Matt 27:38-46, and Luke 23:46)

25. Who's going to get in first — God or Satan?

So the possibility persists that my friends the survivors [of Nazi concentration camps] have so much to teach us *because* of what they endured rather than in spite of it. The value of suffering does not lie in the pain of it, which is morally neutral — but in what the sufferer makes of it. Two persons can go through the same painful experience, one be destroyed by it, the other achieve an extra dimension. The real tragedy of suffering is the wasted opportunity. — Mary Craig.

Suffering can work inside us in two possible ways. It can drive us into a retreat of self pity, hardening our attitude to others and diminishing our interest and enjoyment of life. Or it can have the opposite effect, so that we grow closer to God and perhaps become more sensitive and understanding towards other people. It depends whether or not we allow the Devil to dig his claws into us when we are miserable. Suffering makes us particularly vulnerable to the power of evil, and resentment can easily take root in us if we don't watch out.

If God is to be in the middle of our suffering, it is vital that we hang on to prayer. In acute pain all we can do is make the pain itself our prayer (see Section 24). But there are other kinds of suffering which are not so devastating, but which still wear us out with worry and unhappiness. When family problems grind on for months, or ill health drags us down, we are tempted to abandon everything religious. We tell ourselves that we'll come back to God later, when the problem has gone away. But we must carry on praying *now*, however haphazard our quiet times may be. The Devil's most efficient method of establishing a stronghold in us is to stop us praying. To give up is to cut ourselves off from the source of strength we need most.

Part of praying through pain is accepting it. We get nowhere if we try to ignore our troubles or run away from them. We have somehow to face the truth of our situation and surrender to whatever God will do with us in those circumstances.

'Accepting' is a concept which is easily misunderstood. Some people think Christians are supposed to succumb to all their troubles in a feeble and spineless resignation. This is nonsense. Following Jesus is not the same as being a timid Yes-man. The Christ who went like a sheep to the slaughter is also the Christ who strode through the Temple, sweeping aside the tables of those who were cashing in on Israel's religion. Jesus often made a strong and brave stand for what is right, especially against the Jewish leaders. The cost of this was eventually the cross, which He did accept, totally. *That* is the sort of acceptance we are seeking.

Accepting evil could also seem to blur the distinction between right and wrong. But true Christian acceptance makes us more aware of evil and its power, not less so. If we are going to accept painful things properly, we must be honest about our own reactions. We are bound to protest at first, as Jesus Himself did in Gethsemane. It is far better to pour out our feelings than to bottle them up. But then we have to open up more deeply, letting the pain wash into us, almost relaxing into its blast. If we do this, the pain ceases to be such a threat. It cannot penetrate any further into us, because we have already let it in. By accepting suffering, we reduce its power to twist and destroy us. We can now take hold of our trouble firmly instead of allowing it to master us.

If we pray, 'Lord, I accept this pain; now *You* work in me in all this,' we are opening up ourselves and the whole situation to the powerful love of the Holy Spirit.

Perhaps all this talk about 'accepting' seems to be unrealistic nonsense. If so, we should consider what God does with suffering. In the cross of Jesus, God has taken all our pain and evil into Himself. We need look no further than this if we want evidence that suffering, totally accepted, can be creative.

★　★　★　★　★

I was lucky enough to know Hilary Pole. Her life story has been written in the book *Hilary* by Dorothy Clarke Wilson.[1] Hilary was an old girl of my school when I was a pupil in the 1960s. She suffered from myasthenia, a disease which gradually destroys the use of all the muscles. By the time I knew Hilary she was thirty years old. She was lying in bed, completely paralysed except for a big toe, which was her sole means of communication.

We went in pairs to visit her from school. She was blind but not deaf, so we could carry on a conversation. When she wanted to say something we went laboriously through the alphabet, and she rang a bell with her toe when we reached the letter of the word she wanted to say. Later she had a highly complex typewriter called Possum, which made life easier — at least when Possum worked properly.

Hilary was on artificial heart and lung machines, and was fed through tubes up her nose. She faced endless pain and discomfort, with a frustration that would have driven most people to despair. But..! She was always thankful, concerned about others, and, incredibly, full of fun. When the Minister of Health had been to visit her, this poem appeared on Possum's paper:

> If you wish to cause a stir,
> Make the Sister tear her hair,
> All you need do is relate
> That soon a Minister of State
> Is coming here to visit you,
> Then quietly watch the great 'to do' . . .

Hilary, p202

She loved listening to music and books on tape. A hospital porter who had spent a lot of time with Hilary told us that she had taught him to appreciate classical music. Between our visits Hilary would remember all about us, even though she could not see us.

She was a keen member of the local cricket club, a conscientious Godmother, and a deeply committed Christian. She helped us to see what matters in life.

She died in the early 1970s after a life of unbelievable courage.

I was not close enough to Hilary to know what spiritual agonies she experienced; but she must have known terrible darkness. Nobody could have endured what she did without crying out to God in desperation at times. Yet she took her illness by the scruff of the neck, determined to face it positively. In one of her typed newsletters she wrote: 'It's my body not my mind in bed.'

★ ★ ★ ★ ★

St Paul wrote: *We are afflicted in every way, but not crushed; perplexed but not driven to despair; persecuted, but not forsaken; struck down, but not destroyed; always carrying in the body the death of Jesus, so that the life of Jesus may also be manifested in our bodies.* (2 Corinthians 4:8-10)

NOTES

1. Hodder & Stoughton, 1972.

26. Arms outstretched

He opened wide His arms for us on the cross;
He put an end to death by dying for us,
and revealed the resurrection by rising to new life. —
Third Eucharistic Prayer for Holy Communion, Rite A.

Man is curved in on himself. — Martin Luther.

Picture a man standing with arms outstretched. Because of his position the figure is vulnerable, open to whatever may come of joy or pain. He is giving something of himself by being exposed, but, at the same time, he is ready to receive. This is a parable of prayer.

Outstretched arms are also a sign of reconciliation. After a painful row with someone, we can imagine that we are holding out our arms to the other person. This is often extremely difficult and may take a long, hard struggle with God before we can do it. But there is something powerful in the very weakness and vulnerability of this position which releases a healing energy.

We see our *own* mistakes in the situation more clearly, and the way is left open for both parties to apologise. The chain of hurt for hurt has been broken; that is itself a healing fact, even if the other person does not respond to our attempt to be friends again. The alternative is to barricade ourselves in a cold and impregnable fortress of self pity, as though crouching with fists clenched, ready to get our own back and prove that we were right. If we hide behind our bitter wall of self defence, we cut ourselves off from other people, and from the healing power of God's Spirit. We have created a little hell for ourselves, and imprisoned ourselves there.

To adopt the way of arms outstretched is a risk because we may be wounded again. We might be rebuffed with sharp words such as
'It's too late; the damage has been done;' or

'Yes, and you should have ...' or a grudging,
'It's all right,' which is obviously said with no sincerity at all.
Then it seems that our costly gesture has been useless. Reaching out to
others appears to have failed. Yet it is definitely not failure. Failure
would be to stop trying, and to make our heart into that alluring but
deathly fortress of self justification and revenge.

To live as if with arms outstretched should turn us away from
ourselves and towards God. Then we will find that our praying and
our suffering become inseparable.

The 'word friend' is Forgiven

Someone hurts us by being sharp and irritable. We snap back, and
then regret it. The whole incident leaves us dissatisfied and miserable.
Yet there is something positive we can do. We can take as our 'word
friend' (see Section 6) the tremendous assertion that both we and the
person who hurt us are FORGIVEN. If we are honest, we ourselves
are capable of being unkind and thoughtless as well. The other
person's sin is ours too; we stand together, sinners; yet, in Christ,
forgiven. By using this word friend, and letting its truth soak into our
deepest consciousness, it becomes easier to picture our arms reaching
out towards the person we clashed with.

Jesus Himself stretched out His arms on the cross, to absorb and
overcome all our folly and evil. His apparent weakness was in fact the
greatest strength ever known, because He came through in the
resurrection. Jesus's love and mercy triumphed over all our hate and
sin: 'It is completed! It is finished!' he shouted just before He died.
(John 19:30).

So Jesus's forgiveness is a powerful thing. When we use the 'word
friend' to pray His infinite mercy into our own heart and mind, we are
allowing His healing power to be released into the situation which was
so hurtful. Life does not suddenly become perfect. But our pain is now
a cross-and-resurrection pain, with Jesus at the centre.

The 'word friend' is Forgiven.

★　★　★　★　★

*How blest are those of a gentle spirit; they shall have the earth for their
possession. How blest are those who show mercy; mercy shall be shown to
them; How blest are the peacemakers; God shall call them His sons.* (Matt
5:5,7,9. NEB 1970)

27. 'My cross?'

It is through our lives offered in union with Christ's
intercessory prayer that the energy of the power of God is
both generated and set free for the reversal of evil. —
Mother Mary-Clare.

There is a danger of woolly and sentimental thinking about pain. Some
people refer to every little ache or inconvenience as 'my cross', without
any idea of the enormous significance of those words. Others wallow in
their miseries, hoping to impress everyone by their endurance. To
cling to suffering like that and call it a 'cross' is nothing but misguided
self-centredness. Yet there are ways in which we can legitimately
regard our pain as a tiny sharing of Christ's cross. These are by seeing
the Passion of Jesus in all the agony of the world; and by giving
ourselves to share somehow in His suffering love.

• *1. Seeing.* Christ is not somewhere miles away, watching the world
unscathed from a distant cloud. He has entered and is still entering
into the agony of mankind. 'I was hungry ... I was thirsty ... I was a
stranger, naked, sick and in prison ...' (Matt 25)

When any human being is worn down with poverty, or devastated
by relentless criticism, or forgotten in an isolation cell, Christ suffers
too, with them and in them. 'As you did it to the least of these my
brethren, you did it to me.' And if *we* care enough to be hurt when our
fellow human beings are being hurt, we are one with Christ as well. In
seeing this we take the first step in the amazing vocation to suffer with
Christ.

2. Giving. It is when we have given ourselves to Christ that we can
make a definite link between the things that hurt us and His own
suffering. In spite of all our selfishness, Jesus still invites us to take up
our cross with Him.

But we must beware! We can slip into smug self righteousness with alarming ease. It is not our own virtue that enables us to share in the pain of Christ. It is by the sheer grace of God that we can offer our tiny sufferings to be somehow taken up into His redeeming work in the world. This can never be an automatic process. It is a mystery, which becomes a reality in prayer.

★ ★ ★ ★ ★

Our sharing in the suffering of Jesus does not have to be in outstanding acts of heroism or intense persecution. All kinds of hurtful things can be offered. A shop assistant refuses to join the rest of the staff in stealing small cakes: she is laughed at and isolated as a result. A travelling salesman is unpopular because he won't cheat on the expense account. You organise a party for housebound people and find yourself blamed on all sides for various hitches in the arrangements. You are worn out caring for an invalid member of your family or a handicapped child. Or you are blamed because you defend somebody who is being criticised by everyone else.

Our pain is not ours alone; it is Christ's pain too. This baffling truth becomes our prayer in the suffering.

★ ★ ★ ★ ★

St Paul wrote, *Indeed I count everything as loss because of the surpassing worth of knowing Christ Jesus my Lord . . . that I may know Him and the power of His resurrection, and may share His sufferings, becoming like Him in His death, that if possible I may attain the resurrection from the dead.* (Philippians 3:8-9, 10)

28. Failure. Stand up again!

Then comes the dismal experience of sinfulness and
incompetence, when our spiritual achievements collapse
about us and, like the publican in the parable, we bow our
heads in a plea for mercy . . . (then) it dawns on us that God
is not in our world; we are in His! — John Dalrymple.

Knowing that we have fallen down and sinned yet again is the most
miserable of feelings. Yet it is also an opportunity to grow, because we
come to God empty-handed, in a way that we could not do when life
was going well. It is now, more than any other time, that we discover
our total dependence on Him. This does not mean, however, that we
are grovelling in the mud at our Creator's feet. Our dependence upon
God does not diminish us, any more than a young child is diminished
by her need for her parents.

Obviously we must first face the penetrating light of Christ, so that
His love can burn and purify what is wrong inside us. But then we
must stand up and forget it. After we have gone wrong it is tempting to
dwell on our mistake, churning guiltily over and over it. But we must
let go of our failure. It is finished now, and we were forgiven ages ago.
It is as if God says to us, 'I still love you; I still accept you. Do you
think your sin is so powerful as to stop me loving you? Stand up and
walk. Your sins are forgiven. Does it really matter that your super
image of yourself has been crumpled? Does it matter that your friends
saw you being silly and selfish? The wrong itself did matter, but that is
in the past now. The world has not stopped because you have bungled
things. Stop brooding and taking yourself so seriously. Get up and
dance; have a feast! For you were dead and now you are alive again;
you were lost and now you are found.'

★　★　★　★　★

'I made a mess of yesterday evening. We went out to dinner with friends, and I got carried away exaggerating about someone. What I said was pretty unkind as well. We all enjoyed laughing at him behind his back. I feel ashamed of my part in that now.

'And then I said such silly things — trying to be clever.

'Lord, forgive me. Let the fire of Your love burn away my unkindness and self-centredness.

'Father, I depend on You; I am nothing without You.

'What a comical figure I must have been, all red in the face from too much to drink. Thank you for putting up with me!

'And thank you for friends.'

★ ★ ★ ★ ★

The Lord is merciful and loving, slow to become angry and full of constant love; He does not keep on rebuking; He is not angry for ever. He does not punish us as we deserve, or repay us according to our sins and wrongs. . . . As far as the east is from the west, so far does He remove our sins from us. (Psalm 103: 8-10, 12, Good News Bible)

29. Failure can lead to freedom

God sometimes strips you naked, only to reclothe you in
innocence. — Brother Pierre-Marie.

One of the hardest pains to endure is the feeling of wretchedness and
inadequacy after we have tried and failed in something, especially if
the situation was very important to us. We churn over and over what
has happened, wishing we had spoken or acted differently; we find it
most difficult to accept the fact of our own weakness.

Sometimes all we have to offer to God is our failure. It can take a
while to come to terms with our inadequacy; but if we can see our
failure as a gift that we offer to God in sheer trust, this is a turning
point in the way we cope.

In our unhappiness we can say not only, 'Jesus, I am willing to
suffer with You'; but also, 'Jesus, I am willing to fail with You'. This
may seem an odd way to pray. Yet by the standards of the world the
crucifixion was nothing but a failure. Jesus had not convinced the
Pharisees that his way of compassion was more important than their
rigid adherence to the letter of the law. And He appeared to be just a
deluded religious fool to the cynical Roman military.

On the Cross, Jesus did not only absorb all our evil and sin. He also
entered into the total weakness of failure, losing the communion with
His Father that had been the basis of all His living and teaching: 'My
God, my God, why have You forsaken me?' (Matt 27:46) We could
never plumb the depths of His infinite anguish; but we know that He
has already plumbed the depths of ours.

We also know that Good Friday was not the end of the story, which
is why we can dare to make something positive of our failure. Offering
our weakness to Christ in prayer becomes a kind of dying with Him.
We have to die to all our pride and our desire to be successful and
admired. All we can now rely on, when we feel we have let God down,

is His mercy and love. This brings a new freedom, even though we only receive it hesitatingly at first.

We know that we are understood completely, and that God still accepts and loves us. This is the freedom which enables us to hold our head high, whatever the world may think of us. The pain of our failure does not suddenly disappear, but that pain is now held within something bigger and stronger because it is embraced within God Himself. In a sense, we can now relax. We can stop struggling to be accepted by people or trying to justify ourselves. We *know* that we are the objects of God's love and mercy; that is who we are. Our identity and our peace lie here. This is the truth which makes us free.

★　★　★　★　★

Maybe a teacher's confidence is badly shaken by the failure to cope with a difficult class. Or perhaps parents blame themselves for some painful crisis concerning their children. Somebody who is sensitive and shy may go through agonies after a discussion group, thinking that he or she said all the wrong things. Many Christians are challenged about their faith by friends or colleagues, and often feel that they have made a complete mess of trying to explain what they believe. We all face experiences like this at some time.

It is a relief when we discover that we can offer our failures in prayer, to be taken up into the mystery of Jesus's own redemptive activity in the world; our weakness is offered as a sharing of His sublime strength-in-weakness on the Cross.

We can also offer our inadequacy as an intercession for those who are crushed and desolate, and whose confidence and dignity are destroyed by suffering and cruelty. Our failure thus becomes our gift to God, for them. Praying like this is the foolishness that turns the wisdom of the world upside down — as absurd as the Cross itself!

★　★　★　★　★

My grace is sufficient for you, for my power is made perfect in weakness. (Jesus's words to St Paul: 2 Cor 12:9)

30. Strength in weakness

Do not attach most value to external results, but to being
yourself in the Truth; to being free and at home with
yourself, whatever other people may think. We have been
badly brought up if we always aim at producing an effect on
others! — The Abbé de Tourville.

When we feel inadequate, the people who help us most are the ones
who understand from the inside what it is like to fail. A teacher will be
far more sensitive in dealing with a worried pupil if he has
experienced exam nerves as well. Those who have known darkness
themselves are the most able to listen and encourage others who are
low and miserable. In the same way, our own problems and weaknesses can positively help others. It boosts somebody's confidence as
a parent to discover that *our* children are not perfectly potty-trained
either. People who feel that their prayer is not much good will be
relieved to know that we too have prayer times which seem nothing
but a rag bag of jumbled trivia.

Too much success is bad for us. We would be unapproachable,
almost inhuman, if we were universally popular, brilliant at business,
dazzling at sports and clever in conversation. Deep friendships would
be impossible, and our prayer would be blocked by self esteem. This is
not to say that we should manipulate events, deliberately singing the
wrong notes in a choir, or burning the cabbage on purpose to put our
guests at ease. What we are looking for is a prayerful simplicity in
which we see the truth about ourselves and know that it doesn't matter
when our weaknesses are exposed.

Jesus Himself was tempted in the wilderness to be a sensational
wonder worker. He chose instead the way of apparent failure. In the
end, He accepted such utter humiliation that he could not even carry

His own cross. There is no point of weakness into which the suffering love of God has refused to go. Life in Christ turns worldly standards of 'success' upside-down.

★ ★ ★ ★ ★

In a radio interview[1] Dame Cicely Saunders, who founded the hospice movement, spoke about the inadequacy felt by relations and friends of a dying person. 'But your helplessness,' she said, 'is what you have to offer. You have that in common with the ill person. So you are together with them in that experience. This is what they need.'

★ ★ ★ ★ ★

For the foolishness of God is wiser than men, and the weakness of God is stronger than men . . . God chose what is foolish in the world to shame the wise, God chose what is weak in the world to shame the strong.' (1 Cor 1:25, 27)

NOTES

1. BBC Radio 4, 'Midweek', June 27, 1984.

Part four
What can I offer?

31. Receiving and giving

Perfection consists not in what we give to God, but in what
we receive from Him — St Augustine of Hippo.

We want to grow in prayer; we long to surrender our whole lives to
God. So we ask, 'Lord, what can I give?' And to our surprise, God
says, 'First you must learn to receive.'

We have been entrusted with the incredible gift of life, in a world
full of splendour and colour; we must wake up and welcome it. God's
love is pouring out to meet us; we must open up and receive it.

It may be more blessed to give than to receive. But it is often harder
to receive than to give. If I am ill in bed, I hate having to rely on others
to do the cooking and look after the children. It can be a blow to the
pride to have to receive help. I once stayed with a kind hostess who
thought of my every need, but was incapable of receiving anything
herself. When I gave her a small parting gift she just replied with a
brusque, 'You're very naughty.' The mistake of every Lady Bountiful
is that she gives of her abundance while never stopping to look, listen
and absorb the truth of the situation. She sees the objects of her charity
as 'poor dears', swamps them with advice, and is blind to what they
have to offer.

In all the best relationships, giving and receiving merge into one.
When we share an amusing incident with a good friend, we receive as
much fun as we give in making the other person laugh. Children are
thrilled when they first have some money to spend on presents. They
hide the gifts excitedly in secret places, and then find enormous
pleasure in giving the treasures to us. We receive as we give, and give as
we receive.

If this is true of ordinary contacts between people, it is infinitely
more important in our friendship with God. Prayer is first of all
learning to receive God's love, making space within ourselves so that
we can share in His life. God never forces Himself on us, any more

than He forces us to listen when a wren is singing, or to look inside a snow drop. But to shut down our senses and block our awareness is the opposite of the way of prayer.

As we absorb God's love, and allow Christ's being and words to make their full impact on us, the desire to surrender ourselves to Him follows naturally. Then it is no longer possible to draw a definite line between our receiving and our offering. Prayer becomes increasingly something that God does in us, and we find ourselves giving everything almost before we realise it.

★　★　★　★　★

There is a legend about a holy man who gave up wealth and position to live in prayer and simplicity in the forest. One day some townspeople asked him to come and pray in a church which they had just rebuilt. When he reached the door he stopped. 'I'm sorry,' he said, 'there's no room. I can't get in.' 'What do you mean?' they asked. 'There is a place reserved for you at the front.' He replied: 'I'll never get as far as that. The building is crammed full of words and ideas and plans. Make some space to receive God, and then I will come back and pray with you.'

★　★　★　★　★

I will give thanks to the Lord with my whole heart;
I will tell of all thy wonderful deeds.
I will be glad and exult in thee,
I will sing praise to thy name, O Most high.

O Lord, our Lord, how majestic is thy name in all the earth!
When I look at the heavens, the work of thy fingers,
the moon and the stars which thou hast established;
What is man that thou art mindful of him,
and the son of man that thou dost care for him?

(Psalm 9:1; Psalm 8:1, 3-4)

32. The Devil, the world and the flesh?

In order to arrive at having pleasure in everything,
Desire to have pleasure in nothing.
In order to arrive at possessing everything,
Desire to possess nothing.
In order to arrive at being everything,
Desire to be nothing. — St John of the Cross.

We are faced with a puzzle. On the one hand we are told that the world is God's good gift, which we must receive with thankfulness. On the other hand we are challenged to deny ourselves and turn away from worldly pleasures. How can these two approaches to life be reconciled? Are we to feel guilty every time we go out for a meal? Is it a sin to buy new clothes? Obviously not.

Yet there is an element in traditional Christian teaching which does seem to be extremely stern about material and physical things: 'Every pleasure that presents itself to the senses, if it be not purely for the honour and glory of God, must be renounced and completely rejected for the love of Jesus Christ,' says St John of the Cross[1].

Seen in its right perspective, Christian detachment means enjoying life more, not less. That may seem a contradiction in terms, if we have been brainwashed into thinking that we ought to give up pleasant things just because they are pleasant. True asceticism or self denial is a joyful affair as well as a disciplined one. Saints like Francis of Assisi rejoiced in the world and did not despise it. Their strong sense that everything belongs to God made them call nothing their own. Uncluttered by possessions, they enjoyed creation all the more; and they were gloriously free.

What we are looking for is a mixture. We must be able to stand back, refusing to clutch things greedily to ourselves; yet, at the same time, we must receive life's gifts with a full appreciation of their goodness. These two attitudes do not have to be in conflict. We need both.

If a rose bush in our garden produces a glorious bloom, the last thing we must do is grasp hold of it and crush it in our fist. To enjoy the flower properly we must stand back and let it grow and blossom. If, on the other hand, we cannot be bothered to stop and look at the bloom at all, because we are always in such a hurry, we are missing something that God wants to give us. Christian detachment is *both* the willingness to hold back *and* the openness to receive with our full attention.

God's creation is good, and we spoil it both by greedy extravagance and by thoughtless apathy. We must shake off any idea that Christians should be above everyday pleasures. To reject the world as evil in itself is to deny the essential goodness of creation. God is found in and through the material universe as well as beyond it. Christ became flesh, not a shimmering demigod. The Incarnation of Jesus shows us that life in a human body can be God's life too.

★ ★ ★ ★ ★

The main reason why many classic Christian writings talk about renouncing worldly pleasures is to warn us against being possessed by our possessions.

I once heard about a wealthy couple whose house is full of valuable silver and antiques. The system of burglar alarms is so complicated that their life is made a misery. They have to bolt every window whenever they go out. They are full of fear in case of thieves, and the wife will never sleep alone in the house. So the very possessions which should have been a source of delight have become a heavy burden.

At the other extreme, an American prison chaplain keeps his own house unlocked all the time. He finds the bolts and keys of the prison so oppressive that it is a relief to be totally free of them at home. His house contains many things that are precious to him. But he says, 'If I become so attached to my belongings that I'm afraid of losing them, I shouldn't have them.'

★ ★ ★ ★ ★

Jesus said, *No one can serve two masters; for either he will hate the one and love the other, or he will be devoted to the one and despise the other. You cannot serve God and mammon* [a Semitic word for 'money' or 'riches']. (Matt 6:24)

Paul wrote, *Everything created by God is good, and nothing is to be rejected if it is received with thanksgiving; for then it is consecrated by the word of God and prayer.* (1 Tim 4: 4-5)

NOTES

1. *Ascent of Mount Carmel*, Book 1, Chapter XIII.

33. Giving things away, giving things up

Now more and more there's this Lenten raising of money to
help the poorest. It's growing, and people are beginning to
be more and more conscious that there are in the world
people who are hungry and who are naked, and who are sick
and who have no shelter ...
The new generation, especially the children, are
understanding better. The children in England are making
sacrifices to give a slice of bread to our children, and the
children of Denmark are making sacrifices to give a glass of
milk to our children daily, and the children of Germany are
making sacrifices to give one multi-vitamin daily to a child.
These are the ways to greater love. — Mother Theresa of
Calcutta.

Giving up chocolate for Lent or giving money to Christian Aid is not
an attempt to win a plush seat in heaven; nor will it make us more
virtuous or prove anything to God. It is an outward sign of what
matters in our lives, an acted-out parable of what happens inside us
when we pray. Concrete acts of generosity are not, in themselves, the
essence of the Christian life. But if we try to give ourselves to God and
to be soaked in prayer, so that Christ lives in us, we cannot help but
give away a great deal.

Many Christians are worried by the words of Jesus to the rich young
man: 'Go, sell what you have, and give to the poor.' (Mark 10:21). It is
disturbing to look at all our possessions and feel that we shouldn't own
any of them. We may start to feel uneasy about going on holiday or
spending any money on ourselves at all. We can even become agitated
about household items, wondering if we really do need a colour TV or
an electric blanket. So we worry ourselves into guilt and confusion.

What are we to make of these words of Jesus? Do they necessarily lead us into despair?

It is important to remember that Jesus was giving specific instructions to a single individual, not a crowd. Possessions had probably become all important to that man, a blockage which needed to be removed if he was to be free to serve God fully. So the message of this incident is that we should see if anything prevents *us* from surrendering ourselves to the service of God and of other people. (It might be our possessions or it might be something else.)

This is not, however, an easy escape from the huge challenge of world poverty. We are called to be outrageously generous, and to care even when it costs us a great deal.

There is a tremendous sense of freedom when we realise that everything we have is God's. Nothing is ours to clutch to ourselves; we are simply entrusted with certain resources for the short period of our lifespan. We have to decide how to make the best use of these things. Whatever concrete action we take will reflect our inner attitude to possessions. We give to say Thank you, and to express our concern about others; we do not give things away to avoid feeling guilty about owning anything. We give because we pray, and our praying is part of our giving. Prayer in depth releases the creative energy of the Holy Spirit, who fires the imagination of men and women to find the unselfish ways of living.

★   ★   ★   ★   ★

What, then, should we give up? What sort of acts of self-denial are right for us? We must each decide what makes sense for us. It helps to discuss our intentions with someone whose opinion we respect, a 'soul friend' or 'spiritual director'.

One possible approach is to adopt three 'signs': a sign of sharing, a sign of sorrow, and a sign of thankfulness. These are acted-out parables of our inner desire to use all we have in as loving a way as possible.

A Sign of Sharing: A small, concrete token of the fact that all our skills and time and possessions are God's, to be used and shared as He wants. We could go without butter at breakfast, or give up a meal a week, sending the money saved towards aid for the starving. We could have days of 'simplicity', when we eat only basic foods like bread and cheese, using the money saved in the same way. We could do some 'parallel giving', so that for every pound we spend on something like petrol or meat, we send the same amount to Christian Aid. We could give some hours of our time to a lonely person who needs to talk. We could tithe (set aside for God the first tenth of our money). There are numerous possible ways of acting out parables of sharing; these will vary according to our individual situations.

A sign of sorrow: Many people go without something like chocolate or a pipe on Fridays. This is a way of expressing penitence, a tiny reminder that the sins which crucified Jesus are also our sins. We could drink only water instead of tea at certain times, as a sign of caring about the pollution of our rivers and seas. We could walk part of a journey on which we usually travel by bus or train, sending the fare saved for work among cruelly treated children or victims of war. We could use the walking time for penitence about the violence of the world, and to pray for peace. Possibilities are endless.

A sign of thankfulness: Consciously giving up something which is preventing us from valuing and appreciating God's world fully.

For example: Trying not to go to bed so late, so that we don't miss the freshness and beauty of the early morning;

trying not to have the radio on all the time, because this takes away opportunities for inner stillness;

trying not to nibble during the day, if this spoils our main meals;

trying not to talk so much that we fail to listen and receive;

trying not to watch so much television that we never talk with our family;

trying not to be always in a hurry, which makes us miss so much;

or . . . we know what we need!

Each of these signs is a sacramental action, an external gesture with a hidden, inner meaning. Each one is a way of expressing the love and gratitude and caring which spring from prayer.

★　★　★　★　★

Thus says the Lord,
'Is not this the fast that I choose:
to loose the bonds of wickedness, to let the oppressed go free?
Is it not to share your bread with the hungry,
and bring the homeless poor into your house;
when you see the naked, to cover him?
Then shall your light break forth like the dawn,
and your healing shall spring up speedily.'　　　　　(Isa 58:6-8)

34. It's too much

Forgive us, Lord, when we build worlds which are
dependent on us and not on You. Help us, however feebly,
to realise that the coming of the Kingdom is Your work, and
not ours. — The late Canon Subir Biswas, of Calcutta
Anglican Cathedral.

Sometimes we take on too much. We make ambitious plans about the
money we shall give away or the food we shall go without; and then we
find we cannot cope. Perhaps we feel so tired and drained after missing
a meal that we have nothing left to give our family that evening. Or we
may have given away so much money that we have not allowed enough
to pay for school shoes or car repairs. Perhaps we have developed such
a craving for sugar, having given it up in all drinks, that we are
becoming more self preoccupied rather than less so. Or we may be
spending so much time in religious activities that we never sit down at
home. The sheer strain and weight of what we have taken on becomes
too much. We end up discouraged and irritable, and our inward peace
has vanished.

So we decide to relax some of the demands we had been making on
ourselves. We let go of certain commitments and reduce what we give
away to a level that seems more sensible. Now, we hope, our troubles
will be over. But alas, they are not. A new problem now confronts us:
the destructive feelings of guilt. Pictures of starving children on
advertisements for aid give us an even sharper pang of conscience. We
feel that we are betraying them by making sure that we and our family
have enough.

Challenging words from sermons we have heard ring in our ears.
Are we making ourselves nice and comfortable first, and only giving
our leftovers to the poor? Are we sinking into complacency? Help,
Lord! We are worn out and confused, and worried that we may be

starting on a slippery downward slope.

And God replies, 'Stop trying to take upon yourself the whole burden of poverty and misery in the world. Let go of the soul destroying guilt which makes you think more about yourself than about anyone else. Don't tear yourself apart by thinking that it all depends on you.'

We must face the fact of the world's injustice and agony; we cannot run away from it. But it is God's pain too, and we can share it with Him in prayer.

Being wholly surrendered and open to God is the essential foundation for all our practical acts of sharing. What we give away is the fruit. We must concentrate first on being the plant, rooted and grounded in Christ. The rest will follow.

Be your own guru

Give advice to yourself as you would to someone who has come to you for help. Work out ways of giving which seem best for your situation. Decide as honestly as you can what would be too little and ungenerous, and what would be too ambitious. Seek patterns not padlocks.

Make your promise for a set period, such as a fortnight or a month. Then forget all your questioning and turmoil. Live with that decision as something given. It is there, it is promised. Forget it; think about God instead. Review the situation at the end of the period in case adjustments are needed. And be alert. Maybe God is leading you to a new sort of generosity, a deeper availability to the needs around you.

★　★　★　★　★

In returning and rest you shall be saved;
In quietness and in trust shall be your strength. (Isa 30:15)

35. Having a baby — a parable of grace

*Religious experience is normal experience understood at full
depth. — Professor Jeffreys.*

Having a baby is a unique sort of offering. When a child is born a
mother encounters a whole new world of receiving and giving.
Virtually no other experience is so rewarding and so demanding at the
same time.

In pregnancy the incomparable happiness of feeling the baby
moving inside you is mixed with aching tiredness and often nausea. At
times it takes all your strength to hang on to the sheer grace of God,
because you feel too sick or too weary to give much time to prayer.
'Word friends' are a great help in this wilderness (see Sections 6 and
13).

For many women, labour itself involves the most agonising pain
that we will ever face. Yet the exhausting hours of contractions are
forgotten in the moment of pure joy when the baby is first put into
your arms. This child was carried by you, yet not created by you. You
have been extremely active, but you are also passive, looking in
amazement at this small person who is now going to be part of your
life. It is as if you are at the starting-point of everything that matters.
You have shared in the miracle of creation itself.

Giving birth is a parable of grace, because it is nothing to do with
you and everything to do with you.

The first few days after the birth are a mixture of happiness and
weariness, frustration and exhilaration, all rolled into one. You seem to
spend the whole day (and most of the night) feeding, changing
nappies, talking to visitors, doing scraps of housework when there is a
moment, and wondering when you will ever be able to relax. One
minute you feel bouncy and thankful, and the next you dissolve into
tears because you are worn out and your entire existence seems to have
been sucked into caring for the baby. It is a kind of dying for the sake of

the new life. You are being poured out, almost drained to the last drop, so that your child's life can be established in the world.

Suddenly you realise that you are not free to go out so much, or to do half the things you used to do. You panic and begin to wonder who you really are. This is a new experience of being stripped and pruned; it could be called a supremely creative sacrifice. Yet there will be few events in life which will have given you so much joy.

★ ★ ★ ★ ★

How can anyone live contemplatively when faced with the constant needs of a new baby? All patterns of prayer times fly out of the window for the present. We are lucky if we can sit down for the occasional five minutes with a coffee and 'Phew! Here I am, Lord!'

The whole incredible mixture of receiving and giving can itself become our prayer. We find ourselves in the middle of a life-giving process which comes from God and is soaked in God. All we need to do is recognise Him there, *in* the broken nights and piles of washing, and in the small person around whom the household revolves at the moment. We may need no more than the words 'Thank you' to express everything.

★ ★ ★ ★ ★

Children are a gift from the Lord;
they are a real blessing. (Psalm 127:3 Good News Bible)

36. Praying for others

Intercession is healing. I learnt this in prison from Christ. It must be for those who hurt as well as for those who suffer. Christ does not need our help in the healing, but He *wants* us to share, to give ourselves and to take part in the healing process. We bring them to Christ and let Christ pray in us for them. — Julia be Beausobre.

One of the best things we can do for other people is pray for them. This does not mean trying to persuade God to change His mind about people's fates. We do not have to drag Him into a situation, or urge Him to take an interest in someone. God knows and loves each person more deeply than we could ever do. When we intercede, we are offering to God our love and concern for others. We are making them part of our prayer, and letting ourselves be used for them. There can be no doubt that God always uses these prayers to bless, heal and help people, though not always in ways we expect.

Prayer is primarily giving ourselves to God, not getting what we want out of Him. Nevertheless, there *is* an element of asking in our intercession. It is natural to ask and even beg God to help when someone is in need. At one time I scorned this idea, thinking that intercession was *only* an offering of concern. Then my three month-old son became desperately ill. I found myself kneeling and praying with my whole heart, 'Lord, if I have ever prayed, I pray now. *Please* don't let him die.'

So much for my theory that intercession is not asking for things! In that hospital chapel I was asking God to be there, and for His healing power to work in Andrew. It was a desperate request, offered in the darkness of worry and fear. So when it came to the crunch, asking was my instinctive and natural reaction.

Looking back at that prayer of mine, I can honestly say that it was not an attempt to twist God's arm. I never felt that He was a reluctant deity needing to be cajoled into co-operating. I was pouring out my anguish and fear to God *as my Father,* almost pouring out my whole self for Andrew. I wanted God to be close, to flood the situation with His power and love.

Andrew did recover. We were told afterwards that we were very lucky to have him. I do not understand why my child was healed while others are not. Suffering and death are mysteries beyond our comprehension. But of one thing I am certain. One morning while sitting with Andrew, whose body was a mass of tubes and wires linked to machines, I suddenly knew that he was in God's hands, whatever should happen. I realised that he was loved and held by God, whether he recovered from this illness or not. That was what mattered, more than anything else.

This moment of heightened awareness lasted for only a short time. I soon became distraught again, worrying about Andrew's operation and chances of survival. But that flash of insight was part of my praying, and part of the intercession which lots of people were offering for him. The faith that had come from praying did not take away the nagging pain that I might lose him; but it took away the hopelessness. God was in the middle of the situation, using people to pray His love and healing power into it all.

An increasing number of Christians are being called to a quiet healing ministry, both in physical and in spiritual and mental areas. Intercession makes a tremendous difference in human lives because in praying we harness ourselves with a loving power greater than all evil or pain.

★ ★ ★ ★ ★

After his illness Andrew had several X-rays of his heart. As he was only a baby, I had to stand behind him in the X-Ray room, supporting him under his arms and holding him still in the beam of radiation.

This is a parable of intercession. We stand still, facing the rays of God's love, and hold someone in that beam of light, as I held Andrew. It is a partnership with God for the sake of someone else. Praying for others can be hard work; but that is what it means to care.

★ ★ ★ ★ ★

Jesus said, *You did not choose me, but I chose you and appointed you, that you should go and bear fruit and that your fruit should abide; so that whatever you ask the Father in my name, He may give it to you.*

This I command you, to love one another. (John 15:16-17)

37. Forgetting ourselves, finding ourselves

The essential heart of prayer is the throwing away of ourselves in complete self oblation to God, so that He can do with us what He wills. — Mother Mary-Clare.

Finding God in ordinary life is an idea that has alarmed some people. They fear that the Gospel is being watered down into a cosy, undemanding faith which loses sight of the heroism and cost of true commitment. The concept of 'praying your life' has appeared to suggest that we needn't bother much with God as long as we are vaguely religious in a benign sort of way. This is a complete misunderstanding.

Abandoning ourselves to God at home or at work is *not* a soft option. When we try to live contemplatively, allowing the stillness of prayer to pervade the whole of our life, we discover that everything is asked of us. Whether we are gardening or teaching, selling things or shopping, taking the children out or lying ill in bed, we are called to be completely surrendered to God, and to follow the costly path of loving. This is no comfortable compromise. God is there, all the time, loving us and waiting for our total and unconditional yes.

★ ★ ★ ★ ★

So where am I going?

We sometimes wish we could see more clearly where God is leading us. 'What *is* my vocation?' we wonder. Maybe we hope God has a special plan lined up for us just round the corner, which we only have to discover in order to make everything come right. But for most of us there is no shattering U-turn, at least in our outward circumstances. Life goes on in much the same way, with work and home and family taking up a good deal of our time and attention. There are the obvious exceptions. But we cannot all do the spectacular things. There must be the ordinary Christians, too, to be the hidden salt and yeast of the earth.

To assume that God has a single, fixed blueprint for everyone is to confine Him within our own narrow categories of thought. Such a rigid view of 'God's will' makes many people miserable as they thrash around in their minds asking, '*What* does God want me to do? Surely it must be something more exciting than this. Perhaps I'm on the wrong track; what if I miss the boat altogether and never fulfil God's plan for me?'

It is a relief when we discover that God wants us first of all to be *ourselves*, the person He made in His image. He is loving and calling each of us individually. When we forget about ourselves and about our vocation, and become absorbed in God instead, we begin to find our true selves. *Then* we may see that a certain job or place is where we can most fully be ourselves; that is how a vocation usually comes clear.

What matters supremely is that we love God with everything we've got, in our suburban 'semi', or our convent, or our factory, or our mission station. God says to each of us, 'I have called you by name. Will you let me love you? Are you willing to stake all your life on me?' Our response to this question is the heart of all our praying and all our living.

★ ★ ★ ★ ★

Unless a grain of wheat falls into the earth and dies, it remains alone; but if it dies, it bears much fruit. He who loves his life loses it, and he who hates his life in this world will keep it for eternal life. If any one serves me he must follow me; and where I am, there shall my servant be also. (John 12:24-26)

The last word ... with Charles de Foucauld (1858-1916)

Prayer of Abandonment

My Father,
I abandon myself to You.
Do with me as You will;
Whatever You may do with me,
I thank You.
I am prepared for anything,
I accept everything,
Provided Your will is fulfilled in me
And in all Your creatures.
I ask for nothing more,
My God;
I place my soul in Your hands,
I give it to You, my God,
With all the love of my heart,
Because I love You.
And for me it is a necessity of love,
This gift of myself,
This placing of myself in Your hands
Without reserve,
In boundless confidence
Because You are
My Father.

Acknowledgements

The publishers would like to express their gratitude to the following for use of their copyright material:

Ave Maria Press, Notre Dame, Indiana 46556, USA, for the extract from *When the Well Runs Dry,* by Thomas H. Green © 1982. Used with permission.

Anthony Clarke Books, 16 Garden Court, Wheathampstead, Herts AL4 8RF, for extracts from *Seeds of Contemplation,* by Thomas Merton © 1961; *Revelations of Divine Love,* by Julian of Norwich, translated by James Walsh © 1973. Used with permission.

Dorothy Clarke Wilson, 114 Forest Avenue, Orono, Maine 04473, USA, for the extract from *Hilary* © 1972. Used with permission.

The Clergy Review, 48 Great Peter Street, London SW1P 2HB, for the extract from an article by Wendy Mary Beckett, February 1978. Used with permission.

Darton Longman and Todd Ltd, 89 Lillie Road, London SW6 1UD, for extracts from *The Longest Journey,* by John Dalrymple © 1979; *The Little Way,* by Bernard Bro © 1979; *Julia de Beausobre: A Russian Christian in the West,* by Constance Babbington Smith © 1983; The Prayer of Abandonment from *In Search of the Beyond,* by Carlo Carreto © 1975. Used with permission.

Division of Christian Education of the National Council of Churches in the USA, 475 Riverside Drive, New York, NY 10027, USA, for the biblical references from the *Revised Standard Version, 1946, 1952,* © 1971, 1973. Used with permission.

Faber and Faber Ltd, 3 Queen Square, London WC1N 3AU, for the extracts from the *Collected Poems 1909 1962* by T. S. Elliot © 1970, *Markings,* by Dag Hammarskjöld translated by W. W Auden and Leif Sjöberg 1964. Used with permission.

Fontana Paperbacks, Wm Collins and Co Ltd, 8 Grafton Street, London W1X 3LA, for extracts from *Something Beautiful For God,* by Malcolm Muggeridge © 1972; *The Four Loves,* by C. S. Lewis © 1960; Biblical references from *The Good News Bible* © 1976. Used with permission.

The General Synod of the Church of England, Church House, Dean's Yard, London SW1P 3NZ, for extracts from the Third Eucharistic Prayer in Ther Order for Holy Communion Rite A in *The Alternative Service Book 1980.* Reproduced with permission.

Gill and Macmillan Ltd, Goldenbridge, Inchicore, Dublin 8, for the extract from *Christ Is Alive,* by Michel Quoist © 1970. Used with permission.

Hodder and Stoughton Ltd, Dunton Green, Sevenoaks, Kent TN13 2YA, for the extract from *Blessings,* by Mary Craig © 1979. Used with permission.

Mirfield Publications, Mirfield, West Yorks WF14 0BN, for the extract from *Contemplative Living in the Contemporary World,* by Lorna Kendall. Used with permission.

A. R. Mowbray and Co Ltd, St Thomas House, Becket Street, Oxford OX1 1SJ, for the extracts from *Letters of Direction,* by the Abbé de Tourville © 1939 Dacre Press, A. & C. Black Ltd. Used with permission.

Oxford and Cambridge University Presses, The Edinburgh Building, Shaftesbury Road, Cambridge CB2 2RU, for the biblical references from *The New English Bible,* Second Edition © 1970. Used with permission.

Penguin Books Ltd, 563 King's Road, London SW10 0UH, for the extract from *The Cloud of Unknowing,* translated by Clifton Wolters © 1961. Reprinted by permission.

Ellen T. Ryan, c/o Pontifical Society for the Propagation of the Faith, National Office, 366 Fifth Avenue, New York, NY 10001, USA, for the extract from *Introduction To the Devout Life,* by St Francis de Sales, edited by John K. Ryan.

Dame Cicely Saunders, DBE, St Christopher's Hospice, 51-59 Lawrie Park Road, Sydenham SE26 6DZ, for the extract from a BBC Radio 4 'Midweek' interview, 27 June 1984. Used with permission.

Search Press, Wellwood, North Farm Road, Tunbridge Wells TN2 3DR, for the extracts from the *The Complete Works of St John of the Cross,* edited by Allison Peers, new revised edition © 1953 Burns and Oates; *Self Abandonment to Divine Providence,* by Jean Pierre Caussade © 1972 Burns and Oates Ltd.

SLG Press, Convent of the Incarnation, Fairacres, Oxford OX4 1TB, for the extracts from *Learning To Pray,* by Mother Mary Clare, SLG. Used with permission.

The Society for Promoting Christian Knowledge, Holy Trinity Church, Marylebone Road, London NW1 4DU, for the extract from *The Christian Healing Ministry,* by Bishop Morris Maddocks © 1981. Used with permission.

71250 Taizé Community, France, for the extract from *Letter From Taizé,* February 1984, by Br Roger. Used with permission.

The United Society for the Propagation of the Gospel, 15 Tufton Street, London SW1P 3QQ, for the quote by the late Canon Biswas of Calcutta Cathedral. Used with permission.

Bishop Kallistos Ware for the extract from *Silence In Prayer,* published by the Fellowship of St Alban and St Sergius. Used with permission.

Every effort has been made to trace the owners of copyright material, and we hope that no copyright has been infringed. Pardon is sought and apology made if contrary to the case, and a correction will be made in any reprint of this book.